# Eleazar and
# the Messiah

# Eleazar and
# the Messiah

## Robert Tremmel

*gatekeeper press*™

Columbus, Ohio

Eleazar and the Messiah

Published by Gatekeeper Press
2167 Stringtown Rd, Suite 109
Columbus, OH 43123-2989
www.GatekeeperPress.com

The cover design, interior formatting, typesetting, and editorial work for this book are entirely the product of the author. Gatekeeper Press did not participate in and is not responsible for any aspect of these elements.

Library of Congress Control Number: 2020950050

ISBN (paperback): 9781662907036
eISBN: 9781662907043

# Table of Contents

# Aknowledgements

I want to take this opportunity to personally thank those who have helped me on this journey. My wife Robbie and my children, Julie, Heidi and Matthew are always there to support me and I am particularly grateful to Robbie for allowing me the many, many hours of free time to write this book. I also especially want to thank my daughter Heidi who encouraged me and inspired me with her words, ideas and suggestions. Her insights were invaluable. I'd also like to thank Dr. Janet McCaskill and Carol Donlan who were able to find and correct many of my spelling, punctuation and grammatical errors. There are numerous others, as well, who have supported me in my ministry as a Permanent Deacon and who in many ways, too many to mention, have influenced the writing of this book. I am blessed to have such a wonderful family and so many good friends.

The wise one still seeks him

# Introduction

It's been more than 45 years since I taught my first Bible class in the basement of the rectory of St. Roch's Catholic Church in Flat Rock, Michigan. My wife, Robbie and I, along with another couple, were directors of the youth group at St. Roch. We had no formal training but this was in the early 70's when Pastors were struggling on how best to implement the teachings of the Second Vatican Council. The Baltimore Catechism was no longer seen as the norm for catechesis and, as yet, there was really no solid direction from the Church. Pastors basically "winged it" for more than a few years.

As a result, they had people like us, who were not very knowledgeable about the teachings of the Council, "winging it" as well. In spite of that we had a great group of teenagers led by three of their own under our direction. They didn't learn much, if any, doctrine or dogma, but they did learn how to care for others, be there for others and practice the great commandment to love one another as we love ourselves.

In my first book, "The Four Gospels" I mentioned I had a basic love for the Bible since I was a boy. I studied the Old and New Testaments in college, albeit only a two credit hour class for each. Later, because of a faith crisis, I intensely studied the scriptures for about a year only to discover that for the scripture to really make a difference in my life I needed the gift of faith. Study helped of course but it was faith that allowed me to read the Bible with my heart, so to speak, instead of just my head.

However, even though Paul clearly says it is by faith alone that we are saved, knowledge is also an important factor as we move along on our spiritual journey; especially our knowledge and understanding of the Word of God we call the Bible.

Consequently, I went on to become a Permanent Deacon in the Catholic Church. I then furthered my understanding of the New Testament by pursuing a Master's degree in New Testament studies at St. John's Provincial Seminary in Plymouth Michigan.

For me, understanding the gospels is of prime importance since they reveal Jesus Christ to us. I've said numerous times in my homilies, if you really want to get to know Jesus, read the gospels. It was the primary reason I wrote "The Four Gospels".

I wrote that book with the intention of helping people understand the basic principles of modern biblical interpretation, and providing them with an understanding of the layers of meaning hidden within the gospel stories. My intention was to keep it simple so that anyone could understand those principles and use them to gain a better understanding of the gospels.

However, after talking with many of my readers I found that I did not accomplish those goals. Most of them did not understand much of what I was saying. They said the book was too technical. Many of them didn't understand the words I was using and said I needed a glossary to explain them. I was disappointed but after some reflection I realized they were right. Of course, I had the option of writing a second edition with the hope of simplifying the original but for me that seemed unrealistic. So I decided to publish a new book, this book, which presents the gospels from the prospective of another eye witness - a man named Eleazar.

Eleazar is the Jewish name for Lazarus who is mentioned as a fictitious character in the Gospel of Luke, cf Lk 16:19-31 and an historical character in the Gospel of John. Most of you, I'm sure know the story about the raising of Lazarus from the dead found in the John 11:1-44.

If you read "The Four Gospels" you know that I believe Lazarus is the Beloved Disciple who is mentioned numerous times in the Gospel of John and is said to be the underlying source of that gospel. If that's the case, then he was certainly an eyewitness to Jesus' ministry in Judea. I took the liberty of assuming he witnessed many of the things Jesus said and did in Galilee as well.[1]

I tried to write this book by keeping the narrator, Eleazar, in the background because I didn't want it to read like a first-person novel. Eleazar at times, emotionally reacts to the narrative; therefore, he is able to provide a human connection to the gospel stories. He is my outsider looking in. The scripture tells the real story, and I use footnotes to provide a scholarly explanation of the selected verses, not at the end of the text but within the text. This makes it easier to follow, because the reader doesn't have to keep flipping pages.

Gospel verses are inserted in italics to help the reader easily discern what is from the actual gospels. I also have not followed the order of events as found in the four gospels. Papias, Bishop of Hierapolis in the early second century, said that Mark, who was Peter's scribe, wrote down the words of Jesus as best as he could remember them and not necessarily in the order in which they occurred.[2] So, since we really don't know the order of events,

---

[1] Judea, also called Judah by the Jews, is the southernmost province in Palestine. Jerusalem is in Judea. Galilee is the northern most province in Palestine. Nazareth, Jesus' home, is in Galilee.

[2] Eusebius, author of "The History of the Church" quotes Papias as follows: *The Elder [John] used to say, Mark, in his capacity as Peter's interpreter, wrote down accurately as many things as he recalled from memory- though not in ordered form- of the things either said or done by the Lord. For he neither heard the Lord nor accompanied him… but had no intention of providing an*

except of course that the baptism of Jesus took place near the beginning of his ministry and his passion and death happened at the end of his ministry, I took the liberty to insert the gospel passages where they would be most suited for Eleazar's narrative.

A good example of this is my use of John's Gospel. The Gospels of Matthew, Mark and Luke, which are called the Synoptic Gospels, basically follow Mark's outline of a ten or eleven month ministry of Jesus in Galilee. Much of the material is the same with Matthew and Luke adding some of their own source material, such as the infancy narratives, Matthew's Sermon on the Mount and Luke's parables to name a few. John's Gospel describes a two or three year ministry which primarily takes place in Jerusalem and its environs. I could have only focused on the Synoptic versions, which was my original intent; however, Eleazar is from Bethany, which is only two miles from Jerusalem, so naturally he would have witnessed many of the Jesus events that took place in Jerusalem.

I eliminated much of John's Gospel because, as I stated in "The Four Gospels", I don't believe John's Gospel is historical in the strict sense. I believe many of the words of Jesus found in John are not the words of Jesus in the flesh but the words of the risen Lord Jesus expressed to the prophets in John's community. As a result, those are post resurrection words which were placed in an historical context. I am convinced that Jesus' ministry was longer than eleven months but John's Gospel is more of a "spiritual work", as Clement of Alexandria put it, than historical. For example, Jesus certainly discussed being born from above but not necessarily with Nicodemus or perhaps not only with Nicodemus. He certainly

---

*orderly arrangement of the words of the Lord. Consequently, Mark did nothing wrong when he wrote down some individual items just as he related them from memory. For he made his one concern not to omit anything he had heard or to falsify anything.* Eusebius, Hist. Eccl. 3.39.

spoke with Samaritans although not necessarily in the context of the woman at the well. He certainly was involved with long discourses with the leaders of the Jews but not necessarily in a purely historical context as found in John's Gospel. In fact, I believe, many of those discourses are with the synagogue leaders in the decade John's Gospel was written, i.e. A.D. 90 – 100, with words given to the Beloved Disciple and others by the risen Lord Jesus.

So, I don't use much of John's Gospel because I believe the words of the Synoptic Gospels capture more of the historical Jesus than John. They are also less theological and my main goal is to keep this book simple. I want the reader to get to know Jesus the Son of Man who is Messiah and Lord, and I can think of no better way than to read the Gospels of Matthew, Mark and Luke with a little bit of John thrown in to provide a more balanced view.

Since Eleazar, i.e. Lazarus, is a Jew, I have chosen to use the Jewish names for those who are Jews mentioned in the gospels. It is very unlikely Eleazar would have referred to other Jews by their Latin or Greek names. The gospels use their Greek names because they are written in Greek to primarily a Gentile, Greek-speaking audience. As a result, Simon becomes Symeon, Peter is Cephas, and Mary is Miriam, etc. All Hebrew names that are spelled with a "J" the" J" has been changed to a "Y" because there is no "Jah" sound in Hebrew or even Greek for that matter. Many of the names in the Greek New Testament have been Latinized. Jesus' name in Greek is Yesus; in Latin it is Jesus, in Hebrew it is Yohoshua and in Aramaic, the language the people in Palestine spoke, it is Yeshua. James is Yacob, John is Yohanan etc. You may find this a bit confusing since the gospel texts I quote will almost always use Peter and never Cephas, Thomas instead of Ta'oma, Judas instead of Yudah. As you will see below, all four gospels were written to a predominately Greek audience and Jewish names would have been confusing for them.

You will also find that Eleazar or any of the Jewish biblical characters never refers to God as "God". This is in keeping with the Jewish practice of never saying what is known as "The Name". When God gave his name to Moses in the desert, the text gives us the Tetragrammaton YHWH, which was pronounced only by the High Priest in the temple and only once a year on the Day of Atonement. Since this was limited to the High Priest, and it's been almost two thousand years since there was a Jewish temple, no one knows for sure how to pronounce YHWH. The best guess is Yahweh. Generally the word *Adonai*, "my Lord" is commonly used to replace YHWH in the Old Testament. In the Greek translation of the Old Testament, known as the Septuagint, *Adonai* is translated with the Greek *kurios*, which means Lord or Master. Most Jews referred to God as Hashem which means "The Name" and so Eleazar mostly uses that word in reference to God.

I have tried to base nearly all my material about Eleazar on at least some historical evidence. For example, I say that he is rich, which is based on testimony found in the Gospel of John. He has an above ground tomb, which is usually reserved only for the wealthy. There are leaders from Jerusalem mourning his death and comforting Martha and Mary. They wouldn't be there unless Lazarus was important and, in their culture, social status implies wealth. Making him the rich man who rejected Jesus in Mark 10:17-31 is a stretch but Mark's Jesus looks at the rich man with love and Lazarus, in my opinion, is the disciple whom Jesus loved. I'm not pulling stuff out of thin air. Except for a very few instances, everything I say through Eleazar has at least some validity.

The text contains numerous footnotes which can be distracting. However, you need to read the footnotes as you read the text since they are important to understand the meaning of the text as well as the flow of the narrative.

## The Four Gospels

In order to help you better understand this book, I think a brief explanation of the four gospels is in order.

First off, all of the four gospels were written in what is known as *koine* or common Greek, at least 40 years after Jesus died and contrary to traditional beliefs, modern scholarship claims that none of them were written by eye witnesses. We know for a fact that Mark and Luke were second generation Christians so they certainly were not eyewitnesses. That leaves Matthew and John, both of whom were apostles. However, textual evidence clearly shows they did not author their respective gospels. Scholars also believe these two gospels were written near the end of the first century so it's unlikely they were still alive. That said, it is still likely eyewitnesses laid the groundwork for all of the written gospels, and I think for every gospel an eye witness was the underlying source. Notice it says "The gospel according to…". "According to" does not necessary mean that they actually wrote the gospels. It could simply mean they founded the community from which their gospels came. For example, they preached their version of the gospel of Jesus Christ which eventually was modified and revised to become the Gospel of Matthew and/or the Gospel of John.

So, each of the gospels is a unique presentation of the words and deeds of Jesus. Each one was written for a specific Christian community and each one had a specific agenda that spoke to the needs and issues within its community. Initially, the gospel was an oral proclamation and probably wasn't written down until the eyewitnesses began to die. Now, let's briefly examine each gospel.

The first three gospels, Matthew, Mark and Luke, are referred to by scholars as the Synoptic Gospels. This is because if they are "seen together", the meaning of the Greek word *synoptic*, one finds they contain very similar material which can easily be compared.

## The Gospel of Mark

Most scholars believe Mark was the first gospel written. The first verse, conveniently tells us his theme. "This is the good news of Jesus Christ, the Son of God" (Mk 1:1). He tells us his story is "good news" or "glad tidings" (the meaning of the word, *gospel*) about someone named Jesus who is the anointed one (the meaning of the word *Christos)* who is also a King. Christos is the Greek word for the Hebrew "Messiah". The phrase, "Son of God", likely means a temporal king since the Jewish people called their king, "The Son of God". I say this because Mark does not give us any indication that Jesus was divine.[3]

Mark's Gospel is the shortest of the four and presents us with a very human Jesus. It is divided into two main parts. Chapters 1 - 8 focus on Jesus' ministry of preaching and healing in Galilee, the northern province in Israel, where Jesus grew up. It serves to prove that Jesus was the Messiah. The second part, chapters 9 – 16, focuses on the meaning of discipleship and the portrayal of Jesus as the suffering servant Messiah. This notion is clearly portrayed by the prophet Isaiah, cf Isaiah 52 and 53. Mark highlights Jesus' miracles and exorcisms more than any other gospel. His stories are brief and to the point as are the sermons of Jesus.

Mark was probably written either during or slightly after the destruction of Jerusalem in 70 A.D. Scholars assume this because the author does not seem of be fully aware of it. Also, Mark is most likely the first of the four gospels since Matthew and Luke used Mark as their primary source. Of the 660 verses in Mark, Matthew refers to 600 of them, often word for word, while Luke uses about 60% of Mark.

---

[3]   The phrase, "Son of God" is not found the oldest manuscripts.

As I mentioned above, the Church Father Papias is quoted by Eusebius in his *Ecclesiastical History of the Church*. Writing in about 130 A.D., he said that Mark, who was actually known as John Mark, recalled the sermons of Peter and wrote down the words and deeds of Jesus, as best as he could remember them but not necessarily in the order in which they occurred. Acts tells us there was a John Mark, the nephew of Barnabas, who accompanied him on Paul's first missionary journey. Paul mentions him as a companion in Col 4:10 and 2 Tim 4:11. Peter calls him his son (not as a relative) in 1 Pet 5:13. As a result, most scholars believe him to be the author of the Gospel of Mark. I might add that the composition dates, places of origin, audience and authors are only educated guesses since none of the original gospels were signed or dated. The best scholars can do is take the very limited evidence available and draw their conclusions.

The gospel text seems to indicate that Mark wrote his gospel to the church in Rome. That community had recently experienced the persecution of Nero Caesar, a reign of terror, which led to the martyrdom of many of the faithful. It was a time when Christians, to escape persecution, denied their faith, betrayed their brethren and deserted the community, not unlike Mark's story of Jesus and his disciples.

However, saying Mark is the evangelist is not without problems. For example, he does not seem to know the geography around the Sea of Galilee where Peter lived. If Peter was his source he certainly would have known that. Also, Peter is portrayed in a very poor light. He is not very bright, a braggart and a coward to mention just a few of Peter's weaknesses portrayed in this gospel. Why would Mark, a disciple of Peter, portray his master in such a poor way? Still, the gospel was the primary source for Matthew and Luke, meaning it was held in high esteem. John Mark was not a person who would command such respect. So Peter, based on the testimony of Papias, is the most likely source for the Gospel of Mark.

Ironically, Mark does not have a post resurrection narrative, only the empty tomb. Most Bibles have, at the end of the gospel, up to three resurrection narratives but none of these are found in the earliest manuscripts. The language and style is different from Mark indicating they were added later. Some feel that Mark's ending was lost since the young man at the tomb told the women that Jesus would go before them in Galilee. Since the evangelist knew about this why wouldn't he have added that appearance? On the other hand, Mark could have left it out for theological reasons, the main one being that one must have faith to believe in the resurrection of Jesus.

## The Gospel of Matthew

Matthew is customarily listed first in the New Testament. This is because traditionally it was believed to be the first gospel written. However, as I mentioned above, the evangelist obviously copied from Mark so Mark must predate Matthew. Matthew also knows about the destruction of Jerusalem and describes it in detail.

Matthew is the most Jewish of the four gospels indicating that his audience was most likely Jewish Christians. However, since internal evidence indicates composition well after 70 A.D., these Jews were most likely Hellenized Jews. A Hellenized Jew is one who is religiously Jewish but culturally Greek and most did not live in Palestine.

In addition to Mark, Matthew adds a genealogy (lineage is very important to Jews), an infancy narrative, some parables and long sermons.

Whereas one might say that Mark, with all its miracles, is the gospel of Jesus the wonder worker, Matthew presents Jesus as the new law giver, in a sense a new Moses. Like Moses, Jesus, in Matthew's birth narrative, escapes from the wrath of an evil King. Like Moses he too comes out of Egypt. Whereas the law of Moses is represented by the first five books in the Old Testament, Matthew's Jesus proclaims five major sermons that focus on his interpretation of the law of Moses. This is especially true of *The Sermon on the Mount*, which is, by far the longest sermon, comprising three chapters, 5 – 7. As Moses received the commandments on Mount Sinai, so Jesus gives us his new commandments on top of a mountain. In it Jesus repeats some of the Ten Commandments and rephrases them to reflect his new interpretation. His also gives us the golden rule and defines the commanded to love our neighbor as extending even to our enemies. For him we are to share basically everything with the poor; there is no excuse not to forgive someone and judgement is reserved for God alone.

Matthew's Jesus often confronts the groups known as the Scribes and the Pharisees and Chapter 23 is a scathing condemnation of them. To be fair, these are not so much the confrontations with Jesus in the flesh as they are the community's rebuttal against the Pharisees of the 80's and 90's A.D. When Jerusalem was destroyed by the Romans in A.D. 70 it ended Temple Judaism, the Judaism that Jesus and his disciples practiced. The Pharisees, along with the Christians, were apparently the only religious groups to survive the onslaught. They redefined Judaism as a synagogue experience, condemned the Christians as heretics and expelled them from the synagogue which, at the time, was their normal place of worship. This engendered a lot of animosity between the two groups, and it's this bitterness that is seen in the pages of this gospel.

Like Mark, Matthew does not say or imply that Jesus was divine; however, he is more than a prophet, Messiah and king. Like the prophets he speaks for God but he has also been given divine authority and he is the only one who knows the Father's plan for mankind. While he is certainly the Messiah he is not portrayed as divine since nowhere in the Old Testament or in Hebrew tradition was the Messiah believed to be divine. Kings obviously were never thought of as divine but Jesus' kingdom is of divine origin and, as such, is very different from temporal kingdoms.

Matthew has one post- resurrection narrative, Jesus' promised appearance in Galilee.

Matthew, the tax collector has traditionally been deemed the author of this gospel; however, modern scholarship believes this is unlikely. This is largely based on the fact that the evangelist copied either all or part of almost every verse in Mark. Why would an eyewitness copy from someone who was not an eyewitness? He also relied on a hypothetical document labeled "Q" from the German word, "quella", which means "source". Q contains many sayings of Jesus, many of which are also found in Luke. However, the Apostle Matthew may have been the underlying source for this gospel and may even have been the author of Q.[4]

No one is sure where Matthew's Gospel was written. Some say Palestine, but most believe it was Antioch in southeast Asia Minor, which was at that time the center of the Christian Church.

## The Gospel of Luke

Luke begins his Gospel with the words, "Since many have undertaken to compile a narrative of the events that have been fulfilled among us, just as those who were eyewitness from the beginning and witnesses of the word that has been handed down to us, I too have decided, after investigating everything accurately anew, to write it down in an orderly sequence for you most

---

[4]    Papias, mentioned above, says that Matthew wrote down the sayings of Jesus in his own language which would have been Aramaic. While the Gospel of Matthew contains a lot more than the sayings of Jesus perhaps these sayings, likely Q, is an underlying source for this gospel.

excellent Theophilus, so that you may realize the certainty of the teachings you received." (Lk 1:1-4)

These words tell us that Luke is a second or third generation Christian who is aware of "many" written gospels and wants to set the record straight for a man named Theophilus which in Greek means, "Lover of God". So basically, Luke is a compiler of sources. Like Matthew, he has used Mark as his foundation and added many other sources to complete his narrative including the hypothetical Q source. He also added a genealogy that is different from Mathew's. Some scholars believed Matthew traced Jesus' line through Joseph while Luke traced it through Mary but more likely theological reasons underlie each of them since they both contain inaccuracies. Luke provided his own versions of the birth of Christ and also John the Baptist, plus the well-known parables of the Prodigal Son and the Good Samaritan as well as several other parables not found in the other gospels. He has added material to the passion account which includes the conversation between Jesus and the good thief. In addition, only Luke's Jesus promises to pray for Peter, an angel comforts him in the garden and Pilate sends Jesus to Herod. If we include Acts, Luke has several post-resurrection accounts which include the appearance on the road to Emmaus, the appearance to the disciples in Jerusalem, two ascensions and the promise of the Holy Spirit.

Luke is unique among all the gospels since he also wrote the Acts of the Apostles, and scholars believe Luke and Acts was one book separated sometime in the late second century. As a result, the Gospel of Luke is often called Luke-Acts.

Unlike Matthew and Mark, Luke doesn't focus as much on the end of the world as he does on the everyday experience of what it means to be a follower of Christ. Luke's Jesus is exceptionally kind, compassionate and warm. More than any other gospel, Luke focuses on the care and concern for the poor and the marginalized. His Gospel, along with Acts, has been called the *Gospel of the Holy Spirit* because right from the beginning of the gospel to the end of Acts the Holy Spirit plays a dominant roll.

The author of Luke is traditionally believed to be Luke, a Syrian from Antioch, who was a companion of St. Paul and mentioned by Paul in Col 4:14, Phlm 1: 24 and 2 Tim 4:11. Tradition dates the gospel to Paul's Roman imprisonment at about A.D. 62. However, Luke is very aware of the Destruction of Jerusalem and his description of this event implies that he knows Flavius Josephus' account, which wasn't written until about A.D. 85 - 90. Flavius Josephus was a late first century Jewish historian. So, most scholars date the gospel to around A.D. 85 – 90. Yet Luke says, "Many have undertaken to compile a narrative of the events that have been fulfilled among us…" Who were these many? At the most, aside from Luke, there were only three known gospels before the end of the first century. There were at least a few other non-canonical gospels by the second century. Therefore, I believe the gospel was not written, at least in its present form, until the second century.

Some scholars believe Luke was written in Rome, others say Antioch or some other city in Asia Minor.

## The Gospel of John

John is very different from the other gospels. He follows the general outline of Mark, which begins with John the Baptist, followed by the ministry of Jesus, the conspiracy of the Jewish leaders to kill him, the crucifixion and death of Jesus and the empty tomb. However, only the *Feeding of the Multitude*, *Walking on Water*, *Healing the Royal Official's Son* and the passion narrative are common to both John and the Synoptic Gospels.

While the Synoptic Gospels record less than a one year ministry in Galilee, John reports a two or three year ministry which primarily takes place in Jerusalem. So, it's obvious John is drawing from a very different tradition than Matthew, Mark and Luke.

John's Gospel is divided into two main parts that scholars have labeled *The Book of Signs* and *The Book of Glory*. The former book focuses on the miracles of Jesus and on long discourses primarily aimed at the leaders of the Jews. The latter book centers on what the Evangelist calls Jesus' *Hour*, which is his suffering, death and resurrection.

John wants to show Jesus replaces everything that is Jewish so he has Jesus attending the principle feasts of Judaism and replacing the basic teaching or theology these feasts represent. Other events are used to replace Jewish customs and even their leaders. For example, John's Jesus replaces the light theme of Hanukah because he is the light of the world. He is the Passover lamb since, he is the Lamb of God who takes away the sins of the world. He replaces ritual washings when he changes the water in the vessels used for ablutions into wine. He replaces Abraham because he existed before Abraham, and replaces Moses because, as in Matthew's gospel, he is the new law giver.

John is also combating members of his own community because they have strayed from the original gospel proclaimed by Jesus and the apostles. For example, there were still followers of John the Baptist who insisted John was also a Messiah. There are those who said that Jesus was only human, others, only divine. Still others said he was pure spirit who only appeared to be human. Some also said he didn't really suffer when he died on the cross.

Unlike the Synoptic Gospels, John clearly states Jesus is divine. In the prologue he is called the Word who was with God in the beginning and is the same as God, cf John 1:1. John 10:30 says Jesus and his Father are united as one, and in John 14:8 Jesus tells Phillip that he who sees him sees the Father.

So you can see that John is not only very different from Mathew, Mark and Luke but also a very complicated gospel and, by far the most difficult to understand.

Tradition, going back to Ignatius of Antioch in the second century, states that John the Apostle wrote the gospel. However, modern scholarship indicates it's someone other than John. The Evangelist is very knowledgeable of Jerusalem as well as Temple ritual and worship. His Greek is among the best in the New Testament and his Christology is advanced. It is highly unlikely that this gospel is the product of an illiterate Galilean fisherman.

The gospel itself tells us the author is called *The Beloved Disciple*. As I stated in my book, "The Four Gospels", I believe this person is Lazarus. The gospel clearly states Jesus loved Lazarus and The Beloved Disciple is only mentioned after the raising of Lazarus from the dead. As I mentioned above, a convincing case for Lazarus is made in my book, "The Four Gospels".

John's Gospel was probably written over at least two decades, perhaps even three. There is much repetition, where the Evangelist says the same thing but in a different way with a different theological perspective. Some scenes are out of order as if a portion was inserted without the redactor paying much attention to the flow of the narrative.

Ephesus is traditionally been the place of origin, but some now favor Syria, others Alexandria. I believe the gospel originated in Palestine and then as the community moved away from there it was edited several times to meet the needs of a changing church. The final version of the gospel was probably completed near the end of the first century with the last chapter being added in the early second century by another editor.

# CHAPTER ONE

~~

# John the Baptist

My name is Eleazar[5], the son of Simon Bar Rueben who was a Pharisee[6] and a very devout Jew. He died about four years ago leaving his estate in my care. My mother Hannah died when my youngest sister Miriam was born. Miriam is not married because she brought disgrace to our family and is no longer a maiden but, as we shall see, this was not her fault. My older sister Martha is widowed and childless. We all live together in Bethany, a small village about two miles east of Jerusalem. We are the wealthiest family in Bethany, rivaling even some of the rich families in Jerusalem. I myself am known to the High Priest and many in his household.

My story begins nearly three years ago. It is about Yeshua[7] Bar Yosef, a prophet whom I believe is Israel's long awaited Messiah.

---

[5]   The Hebrew name for Lazarus

[6]   The Pharisees were a religious sect within Judaism which followed the strict observance of the law of Moses, which is also called Torah, and even added their own strict rules mostly regarding ritual purity.

[7]   Yeshua is Aramaic for the Hebrew Yohashua or Joshua in English. It is translated Yesus in Greek and Jesus in Latin. Aramaic was a common

Most of what I have to tell you I witnessed myself. The rest was told to me by others who were part of his inner circle, mostly Symeon Bar Yohanan who is also called Cephas.

> *John the Baptist appeared in the desert proclaiming a baptism of repentance for the forgiveness of sins. People of the whole Judean countryside and all the inhabitants of Jerusalem were going out to him and were baptized by him in the Jordan River as they acknowledged their sins. John was clothed in camel's hair with a leather belt around his waist. He fed on locusts and wild honey. And this is what he proclaimed: "One mightier than I is coming after me. I am not worthy to stoop and loosen the thongs of his sandals. I have baptized you with water; he will baptize you with the Holy Spirit."* [8]
>
> (Mk 1:4-8)

I went to the place where Yohanan was baptizing, a full day's journey from Bethany. It was east of the Jordan River about a mornings walk from the Salt Sea. The mount where it is believed Elijah was taken up into the heavens is nearby. It is a desolate place and the only things that are green are the tall reeds that grow along the river.

I had heard a great deal about Yohanan from the Pharisees who were friends of my father. Some of them thought he was a prophet.

---

Hebrew dialect spoken in many parts of the Middle East in the first century. Everyone from Israel spoke Aramaic. Hebrew, like Latin, was a royal language only used to read the Scripture and also for government and religious meetings.

[8]  Unless otherwise noted, the biblical quotes in this book are taken from *the Revised New Testament of The New American Bible*©1991 CCD, Washington D.C.

As many Pharisees quote the Law and The Prophets[9] they recalled the words of the prophets Isaiah and Malachi:

*Behold I am sending my messenger ahead of you; he will prepare your way. A voice crying out in the desert: prepare the way of the Lord, make straight his paths.*[10]

(Mk 1:2-3)

They said his garb made him look like Elijah and he said he was preparing the way for the Messiah.[11] Some even dared to say he was Elijah who had come back from the dead. But others, especially the chief priests and the Sadducees[12], said he was a false prophet who was misleading the people with the intention of starting a revolt against the temple and its leaders.

The man I saw was a wild man, thin and gaunt from fasting. His hair was in disarray, his beard unkempt. But his voice was

---

[9]   At the time, the Hebrew Scriptures were divided into The Law, The Prophets and the Writings.

[10]  Although Mark attributes this quote to Isaiah, it is actually a combination of quotes from Is 40:3, Mal 3:1 and Ex 23: 20.

[11]  *Masiah* in Hebrew literally means anointed one. There were many different ideas of what the Messiah was to be like. Some believed he was going to be a new Moses, others a great warrior king, few believed he was going to suffer and no one believed he would be divine. The Essenes, sectarian Jews from Qumran, the site of the Dead Sea Scrolls, believed there would be two Messiahs- a priest like Aaron and a king like David. Ironically John and Jesus fit this criterion.

[12]  The Sadducees were an elite religious group of Jews who only accepted the first five books of the Old Testament (called Torah or The Law) as inspired. They were largely members of the temple priesthood and very wealthy. They strongly opposed Jesus and most likely were at least partly responsible for his death.

strong and he spoke with authority. When he spoke you listened for it was like Adonai was speaking through him.

His challenge to repent kept nagging me. As a son of a Pharisee, I always kept the commandments and followed the law. But John wanted more. He said the end of our way of life was coming soon; the Messiah was coming and we needed to be ready. At first, I dismissed his warnings. There were always rumors about the coming of a Messiah and the end of the world as we know it. Since the Maccabean revolt,[13] about two hundred years ago, Messianic expectations have been high. False prophets had led many into the desert only to be slaughtered by the Romans[14]. Was Yohanan just another fake prophet who would lead us to our demise?

I struggled to ignore Yohanan's challenge to repent. Was I not righteous in the eyes of the Lord? My father taught me the law as did the rabbi in our synagogue. I always tried my best to follow the law. I certainly was more righteous than most. Still, his words troubled me. Was I righteous or was I self-righteous?

Yohanan stood in the water and he looked straight at me. It seemed as though he was reading my thoughts. His eyes were dark and deep set. They seemed to look right through me. Quite honestly, the man frightened me.

Then he called my name! "Eleazar, "he said, "come and be baptized." How did he know my name? We had never met. Surely he must be a prophet. I froze. My heart began to beat wildly.

---

13   The Maccabean family led by Judah and his brothers successfully overthrew Syrian control initially under Antiochus IV in the early to mid-second century B.C. which resulted in the first independent state of Israel since King Solomon. It ended when the Romans took control in 63 B.C.

14   The most recent for that time was Judah the Galilean who in 6 A.D. revolted against the Romans and led his followers into the desert to await God's judgement. They were all killed by the Romans.

Beads of sweat ran down my forehead, stinging my eyes. The fire in Yohanan's eyes became even more intense. Then, all of a sudden I felt a great calmness come over me and my fear was replaced with courage. I took off my tunic and walked into the water.

When the Baptist pushed me under the water I could feel the darkness as though I was surrounded by evil. He held me under until my breath began to fail me. I began to panic but he seemed to know this and brought me back to the surface just before I lost consciousness. Air filled my lungs as I gasped for it. I was grateful to be alive. It was as though I had faced death and overcame it. Yohanan smiled at me. "Eleazar, you have been reborn," he said, and he was right. I felt like a new person, free from the guilt of sin, renewed and ready to serve Adonai in whatever way he called me.

As I walked back to the shore to put on my tunic, I saw a man walking into the water toward Yohanan. He was taller than most, perhaps four cubits.[15] His hair was long and a braided pigtail trailed down the center of his back.[16] He walked with purpose and grace. I watched him embrace Yohanan whose eyes betrayed surprise. He seemed both awed and yet somewhat fearful.

*It happened in those days that Jesus came from Nazareth of Galilee and was baptized by John. On coming out of the water he saw the heavens torn open and the Spirit, like a dove descending upon him. And a voice came from the heavens, "You are my beloved son, with you I am well pleased."*

(Mk 1: 9-11)

---

[15]    A cubit is about 18 inches.

[16]    This description of Jesus is consistent with the figure of the man on the Shroud of Turin.

Yohanan held him under the water even longer than me. In fact, it was much longer. I feared for his life and my fears were justified for when he pulled him out of the water his body was limp. He wasn't gasping for air and he wasn't moving. He was dead. Why had Yohanan done this? Surely he must have known he would not survive such a long time under the water. What was he thinking?

Then, suddenly, the man's body jerked violently and he took in a deep breath of air. Gazing up at the heavens he saw something that neither Yohanan nor I could see. He smiled and there was a rumbling sound, almost like distant thunder. Someone was speaking to the man and by the look on Yohanan's face he heard it too. The man turned to Yohanan, they embraced and he left. He donned his tunic and walked off into the wilderness.

> *At once, the Spirit drove him out into the desert, and he remained in the desert for 40 days, [17] tempted by Satan. He was among wild beasts and the angels ministered to him [18].*
>
> (Mk 1:12-13)

I asked Yohanan, "Who was that man?"

He said, "Yeshua Bar Yosef, the one who is to come."

"I thought I heard a voice from the sky speaking to Him," I said.

---

[17]    The number forty is symbolic. Elijah was in the desert for forty days, the Israelites roamed the desert for forty years, and the flood lasted forty days. It most likely symbolizes a new beginning. One could say the Jesus who came out of the desert was not the same as the Jesus who went in. His new life marked a dramatic change from his old way of living.

[18]    Matthew and Luke have much longer version of the temptation of Jesus, cf Matt 4:1-11 and Lk 4:1-13.

"It was Adonai who spoke to him," Yohanan said. "He called him his son, so he must be the one we have been waiting for."

I then asked Yohanan where he was going and he said into the desert to face the evil one. I dared not ask any more questions for I was both disturbed and perplexed by all of this. I went back to Bethany and shared my story with my sisters. They asked many questions but I could answer none of them.

# CHAPTER TWO

~~

# Meeting Yeshua

Forty days later I went back to where Yohanan was baptizing hoping that Yeshua had returned. I met a man named Andreas[19], brother of Symeon and son of Yohanan. They were fishermen from Capernaum[20] in Galilee. It is mostly Symeon who helped me tell this story.

Andreas and I were standing near the shore of the Jordan River and we saw Yeshua walking on the other side. The Baptist pointed to him, looked straight at us[21] and said,

*"Behold the Lamb of God who takes away the sins of the world. He is the one of whom I said, 'A man is coming after*

---

[19] Andreas or Andrew is a Greek name which implies he has Greek roots, somewhat odd for a Palestinian Jew. Perhaps his mother was Greek or more likely a Hellenized Jew meaning she was religiously a Jew but culturally a Greek. The same is likely true of the Apostle Phillip.

[20] John's Gospel says Andrew and Peter were from the fishing village Bethsaida. Mark and Luke both imply that they lived in Capernaum. Both are by the Sea of Galilee so either tradition is plausible.

[21] Other than Andrew, there is an unnamed disciple which manty scholars believe was the Beloved Disciple, cf Jn 2: 35-42.

*me because he existed before me. I did not know him, but
the reason I came baptizing with water was that he be made
known to Israel'"*

(John 1:29-30).[22]

When we heard this we decided to follow him. He turned and, seeming to know our thoughts, he told us to join him. He said he had no place to stay so Andreas invited him to come to his home. It was a long trip, at least four days, but Yeshua said he would be honored to stay at Andreas' house.

Yeshua said he wanted to take the shorter route through Samaria[23]. We were taken aback. Surely he wasn't a Samaritan. Why would he want to be among those who are unclean? Yeshua, again, seeming to know our thoughts, smiled and said,

*"Hear me and understand. Nothing that enters from outside
can defile that person; but the things that come out from within
are what defile."*

(Mk 14-15)

As we walked he continued to teach us.

---

[22]  It seems strange that John says he did not know Jesus. Luke 1:36 says John was Jesus' cousin and John clearly recognizes Jesus in Matt 3:14. This shows us that John is using a different tradition and/or source for his gospel.

[23]  Samaritans were hated by the Jews and vice versa. After the Assyrians occupied the Northern Kingdom of Israel in the 8th century BC the remaining Jews intermarried and mixed their cultic worship with the pagans. Hence the Jews of the Southern Kingdom of Judea considered them to be heretics and unclean. Any contact with them would make them unclean and therefore unacceptable in the eyes of God until certain required ritual ablutions were fulfilled. Consequently, few Jews traveled through Samaria.

*"Is a lamp brought in to be placed under a bushel basket or under a bed and not be placed under a lampstand? For there is nothing hidden except to be made visible; nothing is secret except to come to light. Anyone who has ears ought to hear."*[24]

(Mk 4:21-22)

I thought, "What kind of teaching is this? Why does he speak in riddles?"

He continued:

*"Take care what you hear: The measure with which you measure will be measured out to you and still more will be given to you. To the one who has, more will be given: from the one who has not even what he has will be taken away."*[25]

(Mk 4:24-25)

He knew that we didn't have any idea what he was talking about but he continued to speak to us.

*"This is how it is with the Kingdom of God; it is as if a man were to scatter seed on the land and would sleep and rise night and day and the seed would sprout and grow, he knows not how. Of its own accord the land yields fruit, first the blade, then the ear then the full grain of the ear. And when*

---

[24]   The basic message here is once we have heard the gospel we can't keep it hidden. We are obligated to share it.

[25]   Probably the source of the adage, "we reap what we sow". The more open we are to God's grace the more we will be blessed, not materially as many modern preachers believe, but spiritually.

*the grain is ripe, he wields a sickle at once, for the harvest has come."*[26]

(Mk 4:26-29)

He went on to tell us another parable.

*"To what shall we compare the Kingdom of God or what parable can we use for it? It is like a mustard seed that, when it is sown in the ground it is the smallest of all the seeds on the earth. But once it is sown, it springs up and becomes the largest of plants and puts forth its branches, so that the birds of the sky can dwell in its shade."*[27]

(Mk 3:30-32)

We arrived at Andreas' home that he and his family shared with his brother Symeon's family. We were greeted by Symeon's wife who told us her mother lay sick with a fever. Yeshua asked if he could see her.

*They immediately led him to her. He approached, grasped her hand and helped her up. Then the fever left her and she waited on them.*

(Mk 1:30-31)

---

[26] This probably refers to the final judgement when Jesus returns to separate the good from the bad based on how they responded to the gospel, represented by the seed that is sown.

[27] In the beginning of Jesus' ministry The Kingdom of God was small and insignificant but by the time the four gospels were written and beyond, it had a major presence in many parts of the Roman Empire.

I stood there in disbelief. Who is this man? This woman was very ill, in my mind, almost to the point of death for she could hardly speak or even move. Now she was laughing, preparing a meal and waiting on us. He didn't anoint her with oil or sprinkled herbs on her. There were no long rituals or words to pray for healing. He simply took her hand and she was healed.

Andreas was so amazed he immediately ran down to Lake Galilee to get his brother who was tending to their fishing boat. He soon returned with Symeon. When Yeshua saw him he said,

*"You are Simon the son of John;*[28] *you will be called Cephas"*
*(which is translated Peter).*[29]

( John 1:42)

Symeon cast an impressive figure against the backdrop of Lake Galilee. He wasn't especially tall but he had broad shoulders and big wide hands and large forearms. His hair was jet black, his beard curly and black sprinkled with a little gray. But his speech was that of a Galilean fishermen, heavily accented and crude.[30]

After he changed Symeon's name he told us this parable:

*"There was a wise man who built his house on rock. The rain fell, the floods came, and the winds blew and buffeted the house. But it did not collapse; it had been built solidly*

---

[28]   Mark claims Peter's father was called John, as does John, cf 1:42, whereas Matthew says his name was Jonah

[29]   Cephas is Aramaic for "the Rock", *Petros* in Greek; hence the name Peter. In Matt. 16:18, Jesus tells Peter he will build his Church upon him who is the rock.

[30]   This description is based on a fourth century legend which has little basis.

*on rock. And everyone who listens to these words of mine but does not act on them will be like a fool who built his house on sand, the rain fell and the floods came, and the winds blew and buffeted the house. And it collapsed and was completely ruined.*"[31]

(Matt. 7:24-27)

"Let those of you who have ears understand," he said. But we did not understand him at all. Was the house he was talking about the temple, was it the Israelites, was it the Kingdom of Hashem[32] he spoke about so often, or was it something else? And why was Symeon singled out? Yeshua only just met him. To change a man's name meant he was set apart for a particular purpose.[33] Like his brother, he was an uneducated fisherman. Why would Yeshua choose him to build whatever he was building? Plus, he only just met him. This man was a mystery to me.

Yeshua stayed in Capernaum only two days and then left to return to Jerusalem. He told Cephas and Andreas he would return to make them his disciples. Choosing them to be disciples bothered me. I couldn't understand why he would choose them. They were crude Galileans who certainly didn't follow the law as I did. Why hadn't he chosen me? I was educated and wealthy.

---

[31] The Kingdom of God must be built on a solid foundation if it is to survive the challenges of the world. Jesus apparently sees Peter as a solid leader.

[32] Jews were forbidden to use the word God or YHWH, the name given to Moses. Instead they used Hashem which literally means, "The Name" or Adonai which means Lord, *Kurios* in Greek. Matthew's Gospel, which is very Jewish, replaces the Kingdom of God with The Kingdom of Heaven. Jesus, a devout Jew would never have said, "The Kingdom of God". Most likely he would have said, "The Kingdom of Heaven" or "The Kingdom of Hashem".

[33] For example, Abram to Abraham, Jacob to Israel etc.

I could provide support for his ministry. Certainly, I would be able to understand what he was talking about much better than these two simpletons.

On the way to Jerusalem, Jesus continued to teach me. I asked him what a person had to do to become a member of the Kingdom of Hashem he spoke about.

He said to me, "I tell you Eleazar, no one can enter the Kingdom of Hashem without being born from above."

"What do you mean when you say, 'born from above?'" I asked.

He replied, "Truly, I say to you, you cannot enter the Kingdom of Hashem without being born of water and spirit. Flesh begets flesh, spirit begets spirit. You were born again of water when Yohanan baptized you; now you must be reborn of the Holy Spirit."[34]

"How do I do this?" I asked.

He replied, "Now is not the time or place. You must wait for the appointed hour. Be patient Eleazar. Many things must happen between now and then."

I reflected on all these things. I still didn't understand why he had not chosen me to be one of his disciples. As we approached Jerusalem I stopped and asked him if I could be his follower.

*A man knelt down before him, and asked him, "Good Teacher, what must I do to inherit eternal life?" Jesus answered him, 'Why do you call me good? No one is good but God alone. You know the commandments: 'You shalt not kill; you shall not commit adultery; you shalt not steal; you shalt not bear false*

---

[34]    Words similar to these are found in John 3:3-7 during Jesus encounter with Nicodemus. Surely these words were also said to others. If Lazarus authored the Gospel of John, as I contend, then he was familiar with them.

*witness; you shalt not defraud; honor your father and mother."*
*He replied, and said to him, "Teacher, all these things I have*
*observed from my youth." Jesus, looking at him, loved him*
*and said, "You are lacking in one thing. Go, sell what you*
*have, and give it to [the] poor and you will have treasure in*
*heaven; then come, follow me." At that statement his face fell*
*and he went away sad for he had many possessions.*[35]

(Mk 10:17-22)

I could not believe what he said to me. My wealth was a sign
Hashem was pleased with me; that He was rewarding me and
those who went before me because we were righteous in his eyes.
I gave even more to the poor than Moses prescribed. People looked
up to me because I was wealthy. If I gave everything to the poor
I would lose all respect in the eyes of men. If I gave everything to
the poor, what would my sisters do? How could they live? I was
embarrassed. I had knelt down like a beggar asking for food. What
was I thinking? I looked back at Yeshua as I walked away. Would
I ever see him again? If I did would he remember me?

---

[35] Most people ignore this challenge as being an exception rather than the
rule. Yet the Twelve apparently gave up everything to follow Jesus. Acts
2:42-47 says the early Christian community held everything in common.
The wealthy sold all their possessions and gave the proceeds to the Apostles
to distribute them according to the needs of the community. This socialistic
lifestyle is certainly in direct opposition to the Gospel of Prosperity
proclaimed today by many modern Christian preachers.

# CHAPTER THREE

~~~

# Conflict in Jerusalem

Almost a year had passed since I had last seen Yeshua on the road to Jerusalem. I heard many things about him during his time in Judea. I was told he went back to see Yohanan and actually gathered some of Yohanan's disciples and practiced a baptism ministry. Rumor said he and his disciples were baptizing more people than Yohanan[36]. He also traveled to Jerusalem where he confronted the scribes, the Pharisees and the Sadducees. I heard many marveled at his knowledge of the Scripture but others challenged him, even accusing him of blasphemy.[37] So I decided to go up to Jerusalem for the feast of Pentecost to see if I could find him.

---

[36]   Evidence of this baptismal ministry is found in John 3:26 and 4:1-3

[37]   The Gospel of John tells us that Jesus had about a two year ministry in Jerusalem. The Synoptic Gospels, Matthew, Mark and Luke, relate a ministry of a little less than a year mostly in Galilee. They say he only went to Jerusalem once, the week of his passion and death. John claims he went to all the major feasts and encountered a great deal of opposition there from the leaders of the Jews. This primarily took place before John the Baptist was arrested. All three Synoptics clearly say that what they relate took place after John was arrested. Hence, scholars determine that the length of the

Jerusalem is less than an hour's walk from Bethany. I arrived at about the ninth hour. It was the day before the Sabbath and I was sure Yeshua would be teaching in the Temple area on the Sabbath.

The next morning I went to the Sheep gate on the northeast wall of the temple and I saw Yeshua standing by the pool of Bethesda talking to a man who was crippled.

*Now there was in Jerusalem at the Sheep [Gate]* [38] *a pool called in Hebrew, Bethesda, with five Porticos.* [39] *In these lay a large number of ill, blind, lame and crippled. One man was there who had been ill for thirty eight years. When Jesus saw him lying there and knew that he had been ill for a long time, he asked him, "Do you want to be well?" The sick man answered him, "Sir, I have no one to put me into the pool when the water is stirred up; while I am on my way, someone else gets there before me."* [40] *Jesus said to him, "Rise, take up your mat, and walk." Immediately, the man became well, took up his mat and walked."*

(Jn 5:1-9)

"Was this a trick?" I thought. Did Yeshua set this up to make his followers believe in him. I asked a man next to me who that man was. He said his name was Laban and he had been laying there begging for as long as he could remember; many, many years.

---

ministry of Jesus took place over about three years. It could have been shorter but it could also have been longer. No one knows for sure.

[38]    A word or words in brackets means it is not found in the original manuscript but was likely added by the translator.

[39]    During the first part of the twentieth century a pool was discovered near the northeast wall of the old Temple. The place is called Bethesda and is mentioned in the Qumran copper scroll.

[40]    Legend said that there was an angel who stirred up the pool occasionally and whoever was in the pool at that time would be healed of any illness.

Curing Cephas' mother-in-law was one thing, making a cripple walk was incredible. Who was this man? As I stood there, stunned by what I had just seen, I noticed some of the leaders of the Jews vehemently discussing something with the man who was healed. I quickly walked over there to hear what they were saying.

> ... the Jews[41] said to the man who was cured, "It is the Sabbath, and it is not lawful for you to carry your mat." He answered them, "The man who made me well told me, 'Take up your mat and walk.'" They asked him, "Who is this man who told you, 'Take up and walk'?" The man who was healed did not know who it was for Jesus had slipped away, since there was a crowd there.
>
> (Jn 5:10-13)

They were right. Yeshua had commanded the man to break the Shabbat. If he were really a son of Hashem, he wouldn't have asked him to break the Shabbat. Yet, if he wasn't from Hashem how could he make a lame man walk?

The man left and I followed him from a distance. I saw Yeshua approach him, say a few words and leave. I went up to the man and asked him what Yeshua had told him. He said he told him his name, Yeshua bar Yosef, and he warned him not to sin any more so that nothing worse would happen to him, cf Jn 5:14.

> The man went and told the Jews that Jesus was the one who had made him well. Therefore, the Jews began to persecute

---

[41] "The Jews" is a strange term found mostly in the Gospel of John. Even Jesus refers to his own people as "The Jews". Jesus was a Jew as was his parents and relatives. Most likely, John used this term to refer to the leaders of the Jews who opposed Jesus.

*Jesus because he had made him well on the Sabbath. But Jesus answered them, "My Father is at work until now, so I am at work."* [42] *For this reason the Jews tried all the more to kill him, because he not only broke the Sabbath but he also called God his Father, making himself equal to God.* [43]

(Jn 5:15-18)

Yeshua continued to speak but I could not hear him because the crowds were so large. So, I decided to leave.

The next day Yeshua was in the temple for the feast and he began to teach. The Scribes and the Pharisees were amazed and said,

*"How does he know scripture without having studied?" Jesus answered them and said, "My teaching is not my own, but it is from the one who sent me. Whoever chooses to do his will shall know whether I speak on my own. Did not Moses give you the law? Yet none of you keep the law. Why are you trying to kill me?" The crowd answered, "You are possessed! Who is trying to kill you?" Jesus answered and said to them, "I perform one work and all of you are amazed because of it. Moses gave you circumcision- not that it came from Moses, but rather from the Patriarchs- and you circumcise a man on the Sabbath. If a man can receive circumcision on a Sabbath so that the Law of Moses may not be broken, are you angry*

---

[42] It was a general belief that even though God rested from his creative actions on the Sabbath he continued to rule and pass judgement. Babies were born on the Sabbath, people died on the Sabbath. Jesus' argument is that since he is doing the work of his Father he too can do work on the Sabbath.

[43] John is the only gospel that clearly states Jesus is divine. Yet, calling God his Father doesn't make him divine. We all pray the Our Father and see God as such. John has used this approach to create the ensuing controversy with the leaders of the Jews.

*with me because I made a whole person well on the Sabbath.*
*Stop judging by appearances, but judge justly."*

(Jn 7:15-17,19-24)

His arguments made sense to me. Certainly, it seems that
Hashem would allow someone to heal on the Sabbath especially,
as Yeshua says, it is Hashem's power in him that healed the man.
I wondered why the crowd seemed so angry with him. Did the
Temple leaders and the Pharisees stir them up? They continued to
challenge him as a member of the crowd said,

*"Is he not the one they are trying to kill? And look, he is speaking*
*openly and they say nothing to him. Could the authorities realize*
*that he is the Messiah? But we know where he is from. When*
*the Messiah comes, no one will know where he is from." So Jesus*
*cried out in the temple area as he was teaching and said, "You*
*know me and also know where I am from. Yet I did not come*
*on my own, but the one who sent me, whom you do not know,*
*is true. I know him because I am from him and he sent me."*

(Jn 7:24-29)

Guards came to arrest Jesus but he was able to slip through
the crowds before they could lay their hands on him, cf Jn 7:32.

I made my way back to Bethany pondering all I had seen and
heard. Jesus still spoke in riddles. Obviously, the authorities understood
him enough to want to put him away. But I didn't understand why
they were plotting against him and maybe even to put him to death.
True, he dared to challenge them. They're not used to that. He healed
a cripple on the Sabbath and he said he was sent from God. The
Prophets were sent by God. Was he not a prophet? Some called him
the Messiah. Were they afraid he might want to overthrow Rome and
bring disaster as Yudah the Galilean had done during the census. How
could they overlook the healing we saw yesterday?

I reached my house an hour before sunset. My sister Martha greeted me with a cup of wine and quickly prepared a plate of figs, goat cheese, dried fish, fresh olives and bread. When she asked if I had seen Yeshua, I said yes but did not tell her about the miracle. I told her I did not speak to him, which was true, but I didn't tell her how angry the people were because of his teaching.

One afternoon, my servant Phanuel came and told me I had visitors. I asked who they were and he told me there was a man named Yeshua and two others. Yeshua? I could not believe that Yeshua was coming to my house especially since I had left him alone on the highway outside of Jerusalem. Had he changed his mind? Was he going to make me a disciple? Perhaps he saw me at the festival and wondered why I did not greet him.

I hurried to the front of the house. "Yeshua Bar Yosef, you honor my household with your presence. Shalom," I said.

"Eleazar, Shalom. I would like you to meet my friends. This is Yudah Iscariot and Nathaniel."

Friends? He didn't call them disciples. Were they just friends? If they were his disciples, I wondered, did they sell all their possessions to follow him? Perhaps they were not rich like me and so there were very few possessions to sell.

Yeshua interrupted my thoughts, "You have a fine house Eleazar."

"Yes indeed," I said. It is, by far, the largest in Bethany. "I have two courtyards and the second has not one but two mikvehs.[44] All the floors are made of imported stones and the walls, of course, are limestone hewn and cut near the city. I have an olive grove in the back," I gushed, "and a tomb where my father is buried and,

---

[44]  A mikvah is a stone or tiled pool or tub used for ritual purification. It must be large enough to cover the entire body and fresh water must be used. Most, if not all of the poor could not afford one so they were in a constant state of ritual impurity. Perhaps that's why John's baptism was so popular among the poor. They believed they could be ritually purified by it.

I suppose, where I will be buried one day. I also have many rooms upstairs so all of you are welcome to stay."

"Thank you Eleazar," Yeshua replied, "I am certainly not used to such luxury. Often I only have the ground on which to lay my head. But we cannot stay the night. Perhaps another time.

I was embarrassed. Yeshua had challenged me to sell all of my possessions and now I was bragging about them. My eyes fell but I regained my composure and I greeted Yudah and Nathaniel. Nathaniel was tall and lean like Yeshua but he had red hair and green eyes like King David.[45] Yudah was a short, slender man, swarthy with dark fiery eyes. He rarely smiled and was fiercely intense. "You must meet my sisters, Miriam and Martha," I said.

After making all the introductions, Martha, of course, insisted they stay for supper and began busying herself in the kitchen. Miriam stayed and listened as he taught us about the Kingdom of Hashem.

> …Mary sat beside the Lord at his feet listening to him speak. Martha burdened with much serving, came to him and said," Lord, do you not care that my sister has left me by myself to do the serving? Tell her to help me." The Lord said in reply, "Martha, Martha, you are anxious about many things. There is need only for one thing. Miriam has chosen the better part and it will not be taken from her."[46]
>
> (Luke 10:38-42)

---

[45]    1 Sam 17:42 and 16:12 says king David had red hair and "lovely eyes".

[46]    I call this a reversal passage because it runs contrary to the acceptable and proper customs of first century Jewish society. Hospitality was an important part of the culture. It was also very important in the early Christian community. People were obligated to welcome strangers and provide them with food and even shelter if necessary. The point of the story is twofold: Hearing the word of God takes precedence over all things and women are not only included in the Kingdom but they can also be disciples. Notice Mary is sitting at the feet of Jesus which is the normal posture of a disciple.

As we ate, Yeshua said, "I saw you at the festival. Why did you not come and greet me?"

"The crowd was too big and I could not make my way through so many people," I lied.

Yeshua smiled, "The day will come when you will not be so shy, Eleazar. When my hour[47] has come, you will be the only one who will stand by me. "

He still speaks in riddles. What does he mean by, "my hour"? I dared not question him but it sounded as though I would be his disciple one day. Even Yudah and Nathaniel didn't seem to understand what he was saying.

After dinner, Jesus left with his friends. He promised he would return and visit. He never mentioned my embarrassing plea on the road to Jerusalem. I was again confused. Could I be his disciple without giving up my fortune? Perhaps he just wanted me as a friend.

My sisters were overwhelmed by his presence. "We felt his love so strongly, they said, "but it was not passionate love as between a man and a woman; it was a kind of love we have never experienced before."

They were right. I felt it too. It's hard to describe but it's a love that filled me with great joy, a love that embraced my very being, and made me feel safe and at peace with myself and Hashem.

Yeshua kept his promise and came back often mostly to rest and escape the threats of the Jewish leaders. He told me his arguments with the leaders of the Jews left him exhausted as did the healings. We, along with my sisters, became very close friends. During his visits, he often told us how much Hashem loved us and how deeply he loved us as well. He never brought up the incident on the road to Jerusalem so I decided to let it go[48].

---

[47]  In John's Gospel, "hour" means the day when Jesus is crucified.

[48]  There is no strong evidence that Jesus spent a lot of time in Bethany however the gospels mention Bethany a few times. John tells us there was a

I went up to Jerusalem for the feasts of Passover and Hanukah. I saw Yeshua heal a man who was born blind, cf Jn 9:40. No one had ever healed a man who was born blind. The Sadducees and the Pharisees seemed more hostile with each visit.

Yeshua continued to teach and work signs and wonders in Jerusalem until Yohanan the Baptizer was arrested. Yohanan had made many enemies, especially the chief priests and the Sadducees, because he criticized the temple and its priests. He also criticized Herod Antipas because he married his brother Phillip's wife Herodias.[49] After Yohanan's arrest, Yeshua, knowing he too would soon be arrested, left Jerusalem and went back to Galilee.[50]

---

very strong relationship between Jesus and Lazarus and his sisters, cf John 11:1-43 and 12: 1-8. Matthew, Mark and John all mentioned a woman who anointed Jesus in Bethany. Luke and John both say Jesus' triumphal entry into Jerusalem began in Bethany. The Synoptics tell us, during Holy Week, Jesus left Jerusalem each evening. Bethany is the most likely place he would go after teaching in Jerusalem since it was so close to the city and he had friends there.

[49]   Jewish law forbids a man to marry his brother's wife, even when divorced, if his brother is still alive

[50]   Both Matthew and Mark say Jesus began his ministry in Galilee after John was arrested. Jesus' and John the Baptist's gospels were essentially the same. They both believed in the imminent coming of the Kingdom of God, which would cause a dramatic change in the lives of the Jews. Both appeared to be anti-temple although John more than Jesus. As a result, Jesus' fear of being arrested was likely justifiable.

# CHAPTER FOUR

# Wonders by Lake Galilee

Yeshua began his ministry in Galilee by walking through the streets of Capernaum proclaiming the gospel.

*"This is the time of fulfillment. The kingdom of God is at hand. Repent and believe in the gospel."*[51]

(Mk 1:15)

He then went to Bethsaida and down to Lake Galilee where he encountered Cephas and Andreas.

*As he passed by the Sea of Galilee, he saw Simon and his brother Andrew[52] casting their nets into the sea; they were fisherman. Jesus said to them, "Come after me and I will*

---

[51] The word gospel comes from the old English "god-spell". The original Greek is *euangelion* which means glad tidings or good news and for the Romans it could announce the birth of new heir to the throne of Caesar. Of course, for the disciples, it would imply Jesus was the new king of Israel.

[52] The order of names is usually given according age or importance. In this case Peter is likely older than Andrew and James is older than John.

*make you fishers of men." Then they left their nets and*
*followed him. He walked along a little further and saw James*
[53]*the son of Zebedee, and his brother John. They too were in*
*a boat mending their nets. Then he called them. So they left*
*their father Zebedee in a boat along with the hired men.*[54]

(Mk 1:16-20)

Yacob and Yohanan were also followers of the Baptist. Whether
they participated in the baptism ministry of Yeshua I do not know
but I'm sure this was not their first meeting.

When I heard Yeshua was going back to Galilee I followed
him. I found him in the synagogue in Capernaum and listened to
him read from the Scriptures and teach the people.[55]

*"...on the Sabbath he entered the synagogue and taught.*
*The people were astounded at his teaching, for he taught*
*them as one having authority and not as the scribes.*[56] *In*
*their synagogue was a man with an unclean spirit; he cried*
*out, 'What have you to do with us, Jesus of Nazareth? Have*
***you come to destroy us?*** *I know who you are- The Holy One*

---

[53]   James is the anglicized version of the name Yacob or Yacobe.

[54]   The fact that they dropped everything and followed him is meant to
show the importance of being a disciple of Christ. Leaving everything
behind reinforces the notion of selling everything and sharing it with the
community of faith. As John tells us Jesus knew Peter and Andrew before
he called them. As I said above, most likely he also knew James and John.

[55]   Any Jewish male who could read Hebrew could ask to read the scripture
and preach in the Synagogue. Jesus did this often as did Paul. It also tells us
Jesus was not illiterate as some claim.

[56]   Teachers of that time taught by quoting the teaching of famous Rabbis like
Hillel and Shammai. Jesus did not do this. He spoke as the voice of God
and therefore with authority, cf John 7:16-18.

*of God!" Jesus rebuked him and said, "Quiet! Come out of him!" The unclean spirit convulsed him and with a loud cry came out of him. All were amazed and asked one another, "What is this? A new teaching with authority. He commands even the unclean spirits and they obey him." His fame spread everywhere throughout the region of Galilee.* [57]

(Mark 1:21-28)

Yeshua left immediately. The Leaders of the synagogue, who sat in the front before the chest, which contained the sacred scrolls, didn't move nor did they say anything. The man who was possessed simply walked out almost as though nothing had happened. Others quietly left, the looks on faces betraying shock and wonder.

I sat there dumbfounded. I had never experienced anything like this. I had seen people who were possessed before, nearly everyone had, but I had never seen a demon exorcized. It was frightening and yet Yeshua was in control. He shut the demons up with a mere command and then with another command drove them away. In retrospect, it seemed so simple and yet I could tell Yeshua was exhausted. It was almost as if the demons had drained him of his power. It didn't take long before the story spread throughout the city and beyond.

---

[57]    It's interesting that Jesus' first public cure in the Synoptic Gospels is an exorcism. They are frightening experiences as we can see in the narrative. It's also interesting that the demons in Mark's Gospel always know who he is whereas the disciples, at least at first, never seem to. Jesus' power over evil and his subsequent healings demonstrate that his authority is from God. Only God can overcome evil and both demonic possession and sickness were seen as the result of one's sinfulness and therefore evil. Notice that Jesus rebukes the demon when he names him. Scholars call Jesus' need to hide his true identity *The Messianic Secret*. More on this later.

*When it was evening, after sunset, they brought to him all who were ill and possessed by demons. The whole town was gathered at the door. He cured many who were sick with various diseases[58], and drove out many demons not permitting them to speak because they knew him.*

(Mk 1:32-34)

The scene in front of Andreas' and Cephas' house was chaotic. Hundreds of people gathered there; the lame, the blind and the deaf, those who had stomach issues, breathing problems, and almost every illness one could think of. They were mostly poor; many lived on the streets. He healed them all with simply a word or his touch. I sat under a nearby fig tree wondering who this man was. When we journeyed together back to Jerusalem he seemed like any other teacher. Yet, he was different. There was a certain mystery about him, great wisdom and a deep love for Hashem who he now called his Father[59]. But he laughed and joked with me like any other person. He was so down to earth. But now, I'm finding he is not like any other person I've ever known.

---

[58]  Matthew, Mark and Luke contain twenty five miracle narratives. Unlike John they are very brief and always cause astonishment and wonder. Jesus is often reluctant to perform miracles, I think, because he doesn't want his ministry to turn into a sideshow. Often, the evangelist says that Jesus took pity on the sick person so his healings demonstrated God's love and mercy.

[59]  Jesus used the Aramaic word "abba" when he referred to God. It was not only a convenient way to avoid naming God but also a way to reveal that God was loving and merciful because it literally means "daddy". This was a very familiar term; every Hebrew child called his father abba, but no one ever used it to refer to God. His use of abba in this way must have unnerved many of his listeners, especially the Jewish leaders who would have been very uncomfortable calling God "daddy". Perhaps many of us are as well.

Suddenly, a group of men came carrying a paralytic on a mat. I moved through the crowd to be near the door of the house.

> *Unable to get near Jesus because of the crowd, they opened up the roof above him. After they had broken through they let down the mat on which the paralytic was lying. When Jesus saw their faith, he said to the paralytic, "Child, your sins are forgiven."*[60] *Now some of the scribes were sitting there asking themselves, "Why does this man speak that way? He is blaspheming. Who but God alone can forgive sins?" Jesus immediately knew in his mind what they were thinking to themselves so he said, "Why are you thinking such things in your hearts? Which is easier to say to the paralytic, 'Your sins are forgiven' or to say, 'Rise, pick up your mat and walk?' But that you know that the Son of Man has authority to forgive sins on earth"*[61] *he said to the paralytic, "I say to you, rise, pick up your mat and go home." He rose, picked up his mat at once, and went away in the sight of everyone. They were all astounded and glorified God saying, "We have never seen anything like this."*
>
> (Mk 2:3-12)

The scribes were right, only God can forgive sins. Why would Yeshua say this? Yet, only God can make a cripple walk. Is God

---

[60] The common belief at that time was that sin was the cause of all suffering which of course has its roots in the Garden of Eden story of the fall of man.

[61] Many scholars believe this verse was inserted into the original narrative by the evangelist or someone else to support Mark's theme in verse one, chapter one, that Jesus is the Messiah and the Son of God. In other words, in verse 10 Jesus is speaking to Mark's community and not to the scribes sitting in the house. This is a common occurrence in all four gospels.

offering forgiveness to this man through Yeshua. He certainly made the man walk through him. Shortly afterwards, Yeshua left and went to one of the nearby villages.

> *A leper*[62] *came to him [and kneeling down] begged him and said. "If you want to, you can make me clean." Moved with pity, he stretched forth his hand, touched him and said to him, "I do want to. Be made clean." The leprosy left him immediately, and he was made clean. Then warning him sternly, he dismissed him at once. Then he said to him, "See that you tell no one anything*[63], *but go show yourself to the priest and offer your cleansing that Moses prescribed; that will be proof for them." The man went away and began to publicize the whole matter. He spread the report abroad so that it was impossible for Jesus to enter a town openly. He remained outside in deserted places, and people kept coming to him from everywhere.*

(Mk 1:40-45)

Cephas told me that Yeshua healed a leper. He said the leper came into town and all of them left Yeshua standing there alone

---

[62]  The Bible uses the term leprosy for a variety of skin diseases. While it could be Hanson's disease, it could also be a bad case of acne and everything in between. It was a terrible curse because the person was basically quarantined for as long as the disease lasted. This socially isolated and marginalized the one afflicted. The purification rite by the priest is listed in Lev 13 & 14.

[63]  Here is another example of what is known as the Messianic Secret, a theory concocted by scholars to explain why Jesus wanted to keep his ministry and especially his miracles a secret. I think a simple answer is he didn't want his ministry to be misunderstood. He was not a great warrior King, nor just a miracle worker. He was the suffering servant Messiah who would redeem the world of sin which would ultimately be revealed on the cross.

because they were afraid. It wouldn't be the last time they deserted him. Yeshua stood his ground, apparently showing no fear but his hand trembled when he reached out and touched the man. "When he took off his bandages," Cephas said, "his face was clean and his skin like an infant's.

Cephas also told me some of the Pharisees from Jerusalem had come to Capernaum to spy on him. They had found a man with a withered hand and brought him to the synagogue to see if Yeshua would heal on the Sabbath as he had done in Jerusalem.

> *Again he entered the synagogue. There was man there who had a withered hand. They watched him closely to see if he would cure him on the Sabbath so that they might accuse him. He said to the man with the withered hand, "Come up here before us." Then he said to them, "Is it lawful to do good on the Sabbath rather than to do evil, to save a life rather than to destroy it?" But they remained silent. Looking around at them with anger and grieved at their hardness of heart,[64] he said to the man, "Stretch out your hand." He stretched it out and his hand was restored. The Pharisees went out and immediately took council with the Herodians[65] against him to put him to death.*
>
> (Mk 3:1-6)

---

[64]  Hardness of heart- Often used in the Old and New Testaments, in Hebrew it basically means the inflexibility of purpose and/or perception. In this case it means their stubbornness to be open to the presence of God in Jesus as well as the spirit of the Law of Moses.

[65]  Herodians, in this case, were likely followers of Herod Antipas, Tetrarch of Galilee. Jesus called Herod "that fox" in Lk 13:31 and would not speak to him when they brought him to him on Good Friday.

When I heard they were still plotting to kill him I shuddered. He had left Jerusalem to escape these men. Now they had followed him to Galilee with purpose and resolve to arrest him and put him to death. My whole body trembled, and tears welled up in my eyes by the thought of it.

# CHAPTER FIVE

~~~

# Bethany and Nazareth

It wasn't long after this that Yeshua came to visit. We, along with my sisters, sat in our courtyard and listened to him speak about the Kingdom of Hashem. He, unlike any other man I knew, treated my sisters as equals. For him, they were as much a part of the kingdom as any man and even though my sister Miriam was seen as an adulteress she was welcome. They both were eager to listen to him and marveled at what he had to say.

He looked at us through his hazel eyes, eyes filled with love and said,

… *"Love your enemies, do good to those who hate you, bless those who curse you, pray for those who mistreat you. To the person who strikes you on one cheek, offer the other as well, and from the person who takes your coat do not withhold your tunic. Give to everyone who asks of you, and from the one who takes what is yours do not demand it back.*[66]

(Lk 6:27-30)

"Rabbi", I said, "This teaching is too hard. How can you expect us to follow it?

He did not reply to my question. He simply smiled and continued to speak.

*"You must do to others as you would have them do unto you[67]. For, if you love those who love you, what credit is that to you? Even sinners love those who love them. And if you do good to those who do good to you, what credit is that to you? Even sinners do the same."*

(Lk 6: 28-33)

He paused for a while to let us reflect on his words. He often paused during his discourses to let his words sink in but I think he also used it as an opportunity to collect his thoughts.

This was a hard teaching and I could tell my sisters were having difficulty with it. But he was right. The Gentiles, who are

---

[66]    This is part of what is known as the "Sermon on the Plain" (Lk 6:20-49) and is a short version of Matthew's "Sermon on the Mount" which is found in Matthew 5-7. While Matthew's sermon is longer and includes additional instruction, I'm using Luke here because it is simpler and, as such, probably more original. I believe Matthew embellished Jesus' words to expand his teaching to make it more applicable to his audience. Other parts of Matthew's Sermon are scattered throughout the Gospel of Luke. Both were spoken to the multitudes but no doubt Jesus mentioned these principles many times both in private and in public.

[67]    The Golden rule. A form of this teaching is found in ancient Roman and Greek writings. It is also found in the extra-biblical book of 2 Enoch 61:1. A negative form is found in the *Didache* 1:1, a first century Christian text.

pagans, love those who love them. As the chosen people we must be better than they. Surely Hashem expects that of us.

Yeshua shifted on his seat and continued:

> *"If you lend money to those from whom you expect repayment, what credit [is] that to you? Even sinners lend to sinners, and get back to same amount. But rather, love your enemies and do good to them and lend expecting nothing back; then your reward will be great and you will be children of the Most High, for he himself is kind to the ungrateful and the wicked. Be merciful, just as [also] your Father is merciful."* [68]

(Lk 6:34-36)

"Yeshua," I said, "You can't be serious!" Moses told us to love our neighbor as we love ourselves. That is hard enough, but our enemies? The Romans are our enemies. Surely you don't mean that we should love them?" My sisters nodded in agreement.

Yeshua smiled but it was a sad smile as if to say, "You really don't understand do you?". He shook his head and continued:

> *"Stop judging and you will not be judged. Stop condemning and you will not be condemned. Forgive and you will be forgiven. Give and gifts will be given to you; a good measure, packed together, shaken down, and overflowing, will be poured into your lap. For the measure with which you measure will in return be measured out to you."* [69]

(Lk 6:37-38)

---

[68] The main principle of the sermon is Jesus' teaching about loving our enemies. See footnote on Luke 6:20-49 in *The New American Bible*.

[69] Throughout the four Gospels, Jesus strongly condemns judging others and makes forgiveness mandatory for his followers- two sins of which we are probably most guilty.

Yeshua smiled again and said,

*"Can a blind man guide a blind person? Will not both fall into a pit? No disciple is superior to the teacher; but when fully trained, every disciple will be like his teacher. Why do you notice the splinter in your brother's eye, but do not perceive the wooden beam in your own? How can you say to your brother, 'Brother, let me remove the splinter in your eye,' when you do not notice the beam in your own eye?"*

(Lk 6: 39-42)

I sat there amazed by his teaching. *Who speaks like this,* I asked myself. He speaks with authority and I and my sisters were mesmerized as we listened to him. His words had power and we could feel it but there was something else. Even though I knew I was guilty of the things he had said I didn't feel like he was judging me. I felt as though he understood my weaknesses and that he truly believed I could overcome them.

So I said to him, "Rabbi, how are we to do these things?"

He said, "For human beings it is not possible but if Adonai[70] is with you all things are possible," cf Mk 10:27.

He stood up and told us that he must leave. He hadn't seen his family in a long time and he was sure his mother was worried about him. I asked him if I could go with him and to my surprise he agreed. And so we immediately left to go to Nazareth.[71]

---

[70]    Another name used by the Jews for God. Adonai means *my Lord* or in this case, *the Lord.* In the Greek Old Testament, called the Septuagint, it replaces the Tetragrammaton, YHWH, the unspeakable name God gave to Moses.

[71]    Nazareth was very small town, perhaps only a few hundred families, about 15 miles from the Sea of Galilee and 25 miles from the Mediterranean Sea.

I assumed Yeshua was born in Nazareth but was surprised to learn that he was born in Bethlehem during the reign of Herod the Great.[72] After his birth his parents moved to Egypt and stayed there till he was about three years old. They moved to Nazareth because his mother Miriam's family lived there.[73]

He told me his father Yosef was a builder who worked with wood and stone.[74] Being the eldest son he learned his father's trade and worked with his father in Herod's Antipas' grand city of Sepphoris, only about four miles northwest of Nazareth, which he rebuilt in honor of Caesar. Yosef died in Sepphoris after he fell off a roof he was repairing.[75] Yacob, the oldest of Yeshua's four brothers and his wife Esther took his mother into their house. That was normally Yeshua's responsibility since he was the eldest son, but he said he had a new family to take care of.

---

It rests on a hill in the plain of Esdraelon about 1200 feet above sea level. The rich soil in that area makes is most suitable for farming.

[72] Herod the Great was declared King of the Jews by the Roman Senate and reigned from 37-4 B.C. He was a tyrant, known for his brutality, killing many including some of his sons and one of his ten wives. However, he was a successful ruler and his crowning achievement was the rebuilding of the temple which continued long after his death. After his death, Rome divided Palestine into four districts called Tetrarchies ruled by his sons, Archelaus, Antipas, Philip and Agrippa.

[73] Matthew and Luke's infancy narratives are conflicting. Luke states the both Mary and Joseph lived in Nazareth and only went to Bethlehem because of the census. Matthew says that Joseph had a house in Bethlehem and after coming back from Egypt went to Nazareth because they feared Archelaus, Herod's son who had become the Tetrarch of Judea. Since Luke's version appears to be romanticized and contains some errors, I believe Matthew's version is more plausible.

[74] The Greek word *tekton* often translated as "carpenter" when referring to Jesus and Joseph, literally means a worker of wood and stone.

[75] No one knows what happened to Joseph but he is not present during Jesus' ministry. The general assumption is he likely died some time before that.

What family, I asked?"

He said, "Whoever does the will of Hashem is my family," cf Mk 3:34-35.

We walked silently for a long time until I said, "Bethlehem is the city of David. Do you belong to the line of David?"

"Yes," he said, "Both my mother and father are ancestors of David."

"Perhaps you'll be a king then," I joked.

"Perhaps," he said, but he wasn't joking!

When we arrived in Nazareth we were warmly greeted by Yeshua's family. His mother was almost beside herself with joy as she ran into his arms. Miriam was a simple peasant woman whose beauty was in her smile and deep love for everyone. I have never felt more welcomed as I was by Miriam. She scolded Yeshua because he looked thin and soon set a plate before us that was piled so high with enough bread and cheese, dates and figs to feed ten of us. The evening was filled with peace and joy as we drank wine and celebrated Shabbat. Sadly, it would not last.

The next day, Andreas, Cephas, Yacob and Yohanan joined us and we went into the synagogue.

> *When the Sabbath came he began to teach in the synagogue, and many who heard him were astonished. They said, "Where did this man get all this? What kind of wisdom has been given to him? What mighty deeds are wrought by his hands? Is he not the carpenter, the son of Mary and the brother of James and Joses and Judah and Simon? And are not his sisters here with us?*[76] *And they took offense at him. Jesus said to them,*

---

[76] Roman Catholic and most Eastern Rite churches insist Mary remained a virgin all her life. They interpret "brothers and sisters" as either step-brothers (Joseph's children from a previous marriage) or cousins. Cousins

*"A prophet is not without honor except in his native place*
*[77] and among his own kin and in his own house."[78] So he was*
*not able to perform any mighty deed there, apart from curing*
*a few sick people by laying his hands on them. He was amazed*
*at their lack of faith.[79]*

(Mk 6:1-6)

The people in the synagogue became violent and threatened Yeshua with bodily harm so we left.[80] I found all this hard to understand and as we left Nazareth to go back to his home in Capernaum. I asked Yeshua why they had turned so strongly against him.

---

make little sense since there is a Greek word for cousin and the entire New Testament is written in Greek. Stepbrother is unlikely since some may likely have been older than Mary, plus there is no instance in the entire New Testament where *adelphos*, Greek for brother, is used to mean stepbrother. However, these churches rely on tradition as well as Scripture and there is a second century tradition that Mary took a vow of virginity. Based solely on scripture the best and most likely translation is that these siblings were children of Mary and Joseph. For an in depth understanding of this issue see Fr. John Meier's "A Marginal Jew" Vol. 1, Doubleday, 1991, Chapter 10.

[77]  Notice Jesus, at least obliquely, refers to himself as a prophet.

[78]  There is a common thread in all the gospels that implies and even states the Jesus' siblings did not believe in him, cf John 7:5, as is the case here. While there may have been doubts amongst his kin from time to time it didn't last since Acts 1:14 says his family was a part of the Jerusalem church and James, his brother, became the head of said church.

[79]  Apparently faith is a very important ingredient for healing to occur.

[80]  Luke's version has been embellished and at the end the townspeople try to throw him off a cliff! Cf Lk 4:16-30.

"Because they think I'm a mamzer[81] and my mother is a whore," he said.

I never expected that response. I was afraid to ask him what he meant but, as I thought about it, if they believed it was true no wonder they rejected him. If it were true, how could a bastard ever have the opportunity to learn from the great teachers of Israel? As a child, even the head of the local synagogue would have rejected him. I found my thoughts echoing those of the townspeople in Nazareth; *Where did he get all of this? What kind of wisdom has been given him?*"

---

[81] Mamzer is a Hebrew word which means a person born from a forbidden relationship, e.g., a bastard. It's very likely no one in Nazareth would have believed Mary's story of Gabriel especially since she was a peasant girl. Most would have thought Mary had relations with Joseph before they were married or with someone else. Some would have seen her as an adulteress and likely treated her as such. Jesus, as a mamzer, would have been denied some of the formal training for his Bar Mitzvah and also would have been treated as an outcast.

# CHAPTER SIX

~~~

# The teacher returns to Lake Galilee

As soon as the people in Capernaum heard Yeshua had returned, a large crowd gathered around his home. He led us to a deserted place on the north shore of Lake Galilee between Capernaum and Bethsaida. I had never seen Lake Galilee before I went to Capernaum. It's the largest area of living water[82] I have ever seen, light blue and very clear along its shore turning darker blue and azure as the water deepens.[83] The sand along its shores is pinkish and olive groves and barley fields dot the hills that surround it. It is truly beautiful. At this moment, a light breeze was blowing off shore so the lake was very calm and you could see the hillside reflected in it.

Cephas, Andreas, Yacob and Yohanan had taken one of their boats across the lake to meet Yeshua and when they saw him and

---

[82] *Living water* is a New Testament term for fresh and/or potable water.

[83] Lake Galilee, also called the Sea of Galilee, Lake Tiberius or the Sea of Chinnereth, is part of the Jordan River watershed, the only large body of fresh water in the Middle East as there are very few lakes. It is about nine miles long and five miles wide and about 140 feet deep. It is 650 feet below sea level, the second lowest lake in the world. It has an abundance of fish.

the crowd they brought their boat to the shore. He got into the boat, sat down and began to teach us using parables.[84]

*The whole crowd was beside the sea on land. And he taught them at length in parables, and in the course of his instruction he said to them, "Hear this! A sower went out to sow, and as he sowed, some seed fell on the path, and the birds came and ate it up. Other seed fell on rocky ground where it had little soil. It sprang up at once because the soil was not deep. And when the sun rose, it was scorched and it withered for lack of roots. Some seed fell among thorns, and the thorns grew up and choked it and it produced no grain. And some seed fell on rich soil and produced fruit. It came up and grew and yielded thirty, sixty and a hundredfold. He added, "Whoever has ears to hear ought to hear."*

(Mk 4: 3-9)

He continued:

*"This is how it is with the Kingdom of God; it is as if a man was to scatter seed on the land and would sleep and rise night and day and the seed would sprout and grow, he knows not*

---

[84] A parable is simply a metaphor or a collection of metaphors which, as told by Jesus, is an earthly story with a heavenly meaning. Jesus' use of parables for oral teaching is unique as parables were normally a written tradition. Parables are basically simple stories, drawn from everyday life, that challenge the hearer to search deep within and, with faith, discover their true meaning. The more complex parables such as *The Prodigal Son* have more than likely been allegorized by the evangelist to tailor it for a Greek audience which preferred allegories.

*how. Of its own accord the land yields fruit, first the blade, then the ear, then the full grain in the ear. And when the grain is ripe, he wields a sickle at once for the harvest has come."[85]*

(Mk 4:26-29)

*"The kingdom of heaven is like a treasure buried in a field, which a person finds and hides again, and out of joy goes and sells all he has and buys that field. Again the kingdom of heaven is like a merchant searching for fine pearls. When he finds a pearl of great value, he goes and sells all that he has and buys it. Again the kingdom of heaven is like a net thrown into the sea, which collects fish of every kind. When it is full they haul it ashore and sit down and put what is good into buckets. What is bad they throw away. Thus it will be at the end of the age. The angels will go out and separate*

---

[85] When seeds are used in Jesus' parables the seed represents the word of God so either Jesus or his apostles are the sowers and perhaps also the harvesters although they may also be angels. Jesus tells his disciples that the parables unfold the mystery of the Kingdom of God. Mark's Jesus says the parables are only for the apostles, however Matthew says they are for all those who have faith. This would exclude the leaders of the Jews who have rejected his teachings, cf Matt 13:10-17. The parable of the sower is an example of this. People hear the gospel but depending on the richness of their faith the Word within them either withers and dies or bears much fruit. They fail because of: giving into temptation (the path), inner weakness (rocky ground) or giving into the ways of the world (thorns). Rich soil represents those whose hearts are pure and whose faith is strong.

*the wicked from the righteous and throw them into the fiery*
*furnace where there will be weeping and grinding of teeth.*"[86]
(Matt 13:44-48)

Yeshua turned to his disciples in the boat and said. "Do you understand this?" They all nodded yes but I knew that they didn't. I didn't either. It was only later after his death that my mind was freed from the disillusionment we all had. We were sure he was going to be a temporal king who would call upon Hashem's angels to drive out the Romans and make Israel great again. We did not understand that the kingdom of Hashem was in us and all around us and that it was open to everyone, Gentile and Jew alike. When evening came we sailed the boat back to Capernaum.

*Leaving the crowd, they took him with them in the boat just*
*as he was. And other boats were with him. A violent squall*
*came up* [87] *and waves were breaking over the boat, so that*
*it was already filling up. Jesus was in the stern, asleep on a*
*cushion. They woke him and said to him, "Teacher, do you*
*not care if we are perishing?" He woke up, rebuked the wind*

---

[86]    The first two parables describe the gospel as something of great value which can be found by accident or through diligent searching. Either way, when one finds this treasure, it's worth sacrificing everything to keep it. The parable of the fish has to do with the last judgement, a principle theme in Matthew. At the end times God will separate the good from the bad meting out their reward or punishment, cf Matt 25:26-46.

[87]    Sudden violent storms were very common on Lake Galilee. The remains of a fishing boat were discovered in the Sea of Galilee during a drought and dates to about 40 B.C. It is about 27 feet long and about 7.5 feet wide. A single sail near the front of the boat propelled it. The boat has no keel and a round bottom which would make it difficult to sail in rough water. Such a boat would likely capsize or certainly flood during a violent storm.

*and said to the sea, "Quiet! Be still" The wind ceased and then*
*there was a great calm. Then he asked them, "Why are you*
*terrified? Do you not yet have faith?"* [88]

(Mk 5:345-40)

We were all filled with awe and more than a little frightened by what we saw. How could this man control the wind and sea? Who was this Yeshua from Nazareth?

The next morning, as we were leaving the synagogue in Capernaum, we encountered a tax collector named Levi.

*As he passed by, he saw Levi,* [89] *son of Alpheus, sitting at*
*the customs post. He said to him, "Follow me." He got up*
*and followed him. While he was at table in his house, many*
*tax collectors*[90] *and sinners sat with Jesus and his disciples.*

---

[88] I think this story reflects the persecution of the Church in Rome by Nero Caesar, the community which this gospel is addressed. The early church was symbolized by a boat. Notice Jesus is at the stern by the rudder but is asleep. The words of the disciples echo the words of the persecuted ones in Rome, "Teacher do you not care that we are perishing?" Terrible things happened during Nero's persecution and often the Christians felt deserted by Jesus. Notice Jesus rebukes the wind. One rebukes the devil, not the wind. The Book of Revelation says Nero was considered to be incarnate evil, so rebuke fits. The lesson is that faith is required to still the storms in us and outside us and it's our faith in Jesus that truly saves us.

[89] Matthew's Gospel calls Levi, Matthew, and, if he is the underlying source for the Gospel of Matthew, he is referring to himself. The immediacy of his response is again consistent with Mark's sense of urgency to follow Jesus. Like the four fishermen, Levi probably knew Jesus previous to his call.

[90] Numerous taxes were levied by the Romans. There were direct taxes, land taxes, taxes on produce, road tolls and poll taxes. Individual taxes could also be imposed by cities and then there were Temple taxes. Since there were no graduated taxes, this system hurt the poor the most. Many of these

*Some scribes, who were Pharisees, saw that he was eating with*
*sinners and tax collectors and said to his disciples, "Why does*
*he eat with tax collectors and sinners?" Jesus heard this and*
*said to them, "Those who are well do not need a physician, but*
*the sick do. I did not come to call the righteous but sinners.*[91]

(Mk 2: 13-17)

It didn't bother me that Yeshua ate with sinners. My father, rest his soul, would have been beside himself since Pharisees are very concerned about ritual impurity. But Yeshua had told me that it's not what goes into a man that makes him impure but what comes out of him. Yeshua was not like other men. He had the ability to see goodness even in the most wretched person. He truly loved people and even when he corrected them he did it, not out of anger or bitterness, but to help them understand the will of Hashem. Often, he spoke out against injustice, especially against the poor and there was a lot of that. His anger about such things was righteous because the power of Hashem stood behind his words.

---

taxes were collected by tax collectors known as publicans. In addition to the regular taxes, publicans also charged an additional fee for their services and there was basically no limit on what they could charge. In Palestine many publicans were fellow Jews and therefore hated by other Jews not only because they were extortionists but also because they worked for the Romans.

[91] Jesus often eats with public sinners, something forbidden by Jewish Law. These people were considered ritually unclean and therefore any contact with them would make one ritually unclean as well. One who was deemed unclean could not participate in temple worship. In Galilee there was less concern about ritual impurity than in Judea since Galileans rarely went to the temple. Ritual washings and/or sprinklings prescribed by the Law of Moses or tradition were required to make the person acceptable to God.

On this occasion it wasn't just the Pharisees who challenged him. Others did as well.

*People came to him and objected, "Why do the disciples of John and the disciples of the Pharisees fast, but your disciples do not fast?" Jesus answered them, "Can the wedding guests fast while the bridegroom is with them? As long as they have the bridegroom with them they cannot fast. But the days will come when the bridegroom is taken away from them, and then they will fast on that day. No one sews a piece of unshrunken cloth on an old cloth. If he does, its fullness pulls away, the new from the old and the tear gets worse. Likewise, no one pours new wine into old wineskins. Otherwise, the wine will burst the skins and both the wine and the skins are ruined. Rather, new wine is poured into fresh skins.*[92]

(Mk 2:18 -22)

*While he was saying these things to them, an official came forward, knelt down before him* [93] *and said, "My daughter has just died but come and lay your hands on her and she will live." Jesus rose and followed him, and so did his disciples. A woman,*

---

[92]   Fasting is a time of mourning and would be inappropriate while the gospel is being proclaimed by Jesus. This is a time to celebrate because Jesus, the Word of God, is present in the world. The examples using cloth and wine are used here to show that the new and everlasting covenant proclaimed by Jesus is incompatible, at least in part, with the covenant given to Moses, i.e. the Law.

[93]   In Mark's version, the official's name is Jairus and he is a synagogue official, obviously a Jew. Here, he doesn't kneel but prostrates himself before Jesus, the typical posture of a Jew desperately asking for help. The differences in similar stories by different evangelists indicate that, many of the stories are written down from memory and/or edited. To compare, cf Mk 5:21 – 43.

*suffering from hemorrhages for twelve years, came up behind him, and touched the tassel on his cloak. She said to herself, "If only I can touch his cloak, I shall be cured." Jesus turned around and saw her and said, "Courage daughter! Your faith has saved you." And from that hour the woman was cured.*[94]

*When Jesus arrived at the official's house and saw the flute players and the crowd, he said, "Go away! The girl is not dead but sleeping." And they ridiculed him. When the crowd was put out, he came and took her by the hand, and the little girl arose. The news of this spread throughout the land.*

*(Matt 9:18 -26)*

Cephas told me the official's name was Yairus. Cephas, Yacob and Yohanan had witnessed both miracles, first hand. Frankly, I did not believe that Yeshua had raised the girl from the dead. No one can raise someone from the dead. "She must have been in a trance or a coma," I said. Cephas insisted the girl was dead and that Yeshua has raised her by simply taking her by the hand telling her to rise. I insisted she was not dead; she just appeared dead. One day I myself would experience Yeshua's power to raise the dead in an even more powerful way than Yairus' daughter.

---

[94]  The woman, because she has been in contact with blood for twelve years has been ritually impure for twelve years. She is taking a big risk by going out in the crowd because everyone she touches will become ritually impure. If she is found out, her punishment could be severe. But, her faith in Jesus tells her it's worth the risk and, as Jesus says, it's her faith that has saved her. The Greek word used here for "save" means "to become whole or complete" meaning she has been healed not only physically but also mentally and spiritually as well.

## CHAPTER SEVEN

~~~

# Yeshua chooses his emissaries

Yeshua continued to have more followers especially since news of his miracles had spread throughout Galilee. Aside from the crowds that followed him, there were over thirty of us who almost always were with him. One day he took us to the top of Mt Tabor. Mt Tabor is an unusual formation that rises directly out the flat plains around it. It is almost 2000 feet high so you can easily see the Sea of Galilee as well as the Great Sea[95] from it. It is truly breathtaking. There he appointed twelve men whom he called Messengers.[96]

*He went up to the mountain and summoned those whom he wanted and they came to him. He appointed twelve [97] [whom he also named apostles] that they might be with him and he sent them forth to preach and to have authority to drive out demons:*

---

[95] The first century name for the Mediterranean Sea

[96] The meaning of the word *apostle*.

[97] "Twelve is likely a symbolic number representing the twelve tribes of Israel and could mean that Jesus was establishing a new Israel. His followers likely would have taken it that way, which for some, if not many, he would have been seen as a warrior king like David.

*he appointed the twelve: Simon whom he named Peter, James, the*
*son of Zebedee, and John the brother of James, whom he named*
*Boanerges, that is son of thunder; Andrew, Philip, Bartholomew,*
*Matthew, Thomas, James the son of Alphaeus, Thaddeus, Simon*
*the Cananean and Judas Iscariot who betrayed him.*[98]

(Mk 3: 13-19)

I didn't understand why Yeshua didn't choose me to be among the Twelve. Except for Yudah Iscariot and Levi, they were illiterate peasants, crude Galileans, buffoons. I was learned. I could read Hebrew and Aramaic and even a little Greek. And I could write because, as a youth, I wanted to follow in my father's footsteps so I studied to be a scribe.[99] I asked Yeshua why I was not chosen. He smiled and looked at me with love. He told me that his Father had other plans for me. "Your hour has not yet come Eleazar but you will surely know when it does," he said.

There was a nice grassy area at the top of Tabor where Yeshua told us to sit down. When we were comfortable, he also sat down on the grass and he began to teach us saying:

*"Blessed are the poor in spirit*[100] *for theirs is the kingdom of heaven.*
*Blessed are they who mourn, for they shall be comforted.*

---

[98]   Peter is first on all the lists of the Twelve Apostles indicating that he is the most important, not necessary at the time he was called but rather by the time the gospels were written down. Judas is always last and almost always is referred to in all the gospels as Jesus' betrayer.

[99]   Scribes were distinguished scholars who were often fluent in the Law of Moses, i.e. Torah. They were copiers of the Law and the Prophets and also drew up legal documents. Some of the Pharisees apparently were also scribes.

[100]   Mostly this means those who recognized their need for God or it could simply mean, humble.

*Blessed are the meek for they will inherit the land.*

*Blessed are they who thirst for righteousness*[101] *for they will be satisfied.*

*Blessed are the merciful for they will be shown mercy.*

*Blessed are the clean of heart,*[102] *for they will see God.*

*Blessed are the peacemakers for they shall be called the children of God.*

*Blessed are they who are persecuted for the sake of righteousness for theirs is the kingdom of heaven.*

*Blessed are you when they insult you and persecute you and utter every kind of slander against you [falsely] because of me. Rejoice and be glad, for your reward will be great in heaven. Thus, they persecuted the prophets who were born before you.*"[103]

(Matt 5:1-12)

---

[101] Those who understand and conform to God's will

[102] Those who are without guile

[103] Often called the nine beatitudes, this poem serves as an introduction to what scholars call the Sermon on the Mount. I believe they are the description of the perfect disciple because they epitomize everything Jesus is and what a true disciple should be like. Luke only has four beatitudes which are followed by four woes contrasting the dramatic social differences between the poor and the wealthy in Israel. The word in Greek for blessed is *makarioi* which literally means "Fortunate". For Jesus the truly fortunate were not those who had money or status but those who know and do God's will. As Jesus tells us later in the Sermon on the Mount, true wealth comes from within. Most likely Luke's simpler version is closer to the words of Jesus. Matthew expanded Luke's source, called "Q' by scholars, to fit his agenda and make it more appropriate for his Hellenized Jewish audience. It is unlikely Jesus said all the words found in the Sermon, which covers three chapters, at one time. Matthew simply compiled the teachings of Jesus into one setting to condense them and make them easier to remember.

These teachings are so different than those of the Scribes and the Pharisees. They, of course, teach us to care for the poor, the widow and the orphan because such direction is found in the Torah but they also teach that wealth is a gift from God. It's God's reward for being good and following the Law. For Yeshua, it's the poor who will inherit the kingdom. Where does that leave me? I'm now sure that's why Yeshua told me to sell everything I have and give it to the poor. How can I be saved?

But, what about Matthew? He is wealthy and his wealth was obtained by treachery and extortion. Surely, I am better than he. Unlike those crazy Zealots I desire peace. Symeon is a Zealot. How can he be a part of the Kingdom? And Yohanan, Zebedee's son; he's constantly losing his temper. He creates chaos not peace. I could have gone on but I looked at Yeshua who gave me that knowing smile. He called Pharisees hypocrites. I was a Pharisee's son. Perhaps I wasn't fit to be his disciple.

Yeshua continued to teach us.

*"You are the salt of the earth. But if the salt loses its taste, with what can it be seasoned?* [104] *It is no longer good for anything but to be thrown out and trampled underfoot. You are the light of the world. A city set on a mountain cannot be hidden. Nor do you light a lamp and then put it under a bushel basket; it is set on a lampstand, where it gives light to the whole house. Just so, your light must shine before others, that they may see your good deeds and glorify your heavenly Father.*

(Matt 5:13-16)

---

[104] Salt really never loses its flavor. However, in Israel the people used to put crude rock salt into a bag and hang the bag in the pot in which they were cooking their food. The salt would eventually dissolve and the remaining debris would be thrown outside to be "trampled underfoot".

Yacob asked Yeshua to teach us how to pray.

*"When you pray, do not be like the hypocrites, who love to stand and pray in the synagogues and on the street corners so that others may see them. Amen, I say to you, they have received their reward. But when you pray, go into your room, close the door and pray to your Father in secret. And your Father, who sees in secret, will repay you.*

*In praying, do not babble like the pagans, who think that they will be heard because of their many words. Do not be like them. Your Father knows what you need before you ask him."*

(Matt 6:5-8)

He continued:

*"When you pray say: Father, hallowed be your name, your kingdom come. Give us each day our daily bread and forgive us our sins. For we ourselves forgive everyone in debt to us, and do not subject us to the final test."*[105]

(Lk 11:2-4)

My father was a hypocrite? He used to dress up in his most expensive attire to go to the Temple to pray. He'd stand there in the morning with his phylacteries[106] hanging from his hat and

---

[105] I chose to use Luke's version of the Our Father since it is simpler and usually simpler means it's probably closer to the original. The final test refers to the end times. This part of the prayer asks God to spare them from the calamities foretold about the second coming and the end of the world as we know it.

[106] Small leather receptacles that contained small strips of parchment with quotes from the Book of Deuteronomy reminded them of their obligation to keep the Law. In Hebrew they were called *teffilin*. Phylactery in Greek means amulet.

right arm raising his arms in prayer, reciting the Psalms and verses from the Law.

Yet, I never saw Yeshua pray this way. He'd often go out to a quiet place in the evening to pray, sometimes all night. Once, I sneaked out to hear him pray and he barely spoke. Mostly, he just sat on the ground with his arms raised in prayer but with no words. The look on his face was ecstatic and his face shone with such brilliance it lit up the area where he sat. I was stunned and a little frightened so I never went back.

Perhaps that's why the prayer he taught us was so simple. He praised his Abba, asked him to send his kingdom, provide us with basic needs and then warning that we must forgive others as the Father forgive us and finally asking Hashem to be merciful. We all expected something more; something much more and yet it was really all we needed to say as long as we said it from our hearts and not just our lips.

We came down from the mountain and travelled back through the towns and villages in Galilee.

*He went around all of Galilee, teaching in their synagogues, proclaiming the gospel of the kingdom and curing every disease and illness among the people. His fame spread to all of Syria and they brought him all who were sick with various diseases and racked with pain, those who were possessed, lunatics, and paralytics and he cured them. And great crowds from Galilee, the Decapolis,[107] Jerusalem, and Judea, and from beyond the Jordan followed him."*

(Matt 4:23-25)

---

[107] From the Greek, *deka* and *polis* it means ten cities. These Gentile cities were founded by Alexander the Great in 323 B.C. and occupied an area east of the Jordan River.

~~~

# CHAPTER EIGHT

# The Baptist dies and the crowds fed

The crowds remained overnight and again he began to heal them until messengers came with some very disturbing news.

*Now Herod had arrested John, bound him and put him into prison on account of Herodias, the wife of his brother Philip, for John had said to him, "It is not lawful for you to have her." Although, he wanted to kill him, he feared the people, for they regarded him as a prophet. But at a birthday celebration for Herod, the daughter of Herodias performed a dance before the guests and delighted Herod so much that he swore to give her whatever she might ask for. Prompted by her mother, she said, "Give me here on a platter the head of John the Baptist." The king was distressed, but because of his oaths and the guests who were present, he ordered that it be given, and he had John beheaded in prison. His head was brought in on a platter and given to the girl, who took it to her mother. His disciples came and took away the corpse and buried him; and they went and told Jesus.*[108]

(Matt 14:3-12)

When Yeshua heard this he was deeply troubled and began to speak to the crowds about Yohanan.

*"What did you go out to the desert to see? A reed swayed by the wind? Then, what did you go out to see? Someone dressed in fine clothing? Those who wear fine clothing are in royal palaces. Then why did you go out? To see a prophet? Yes, I tell you, and more than prophet. This is the one about whom it is written:*

*'Behold, I am sending my messenger*
*ahead of you;*
*He will prepare your way before you.'*

*Amen, I say to you, among those born of women there is none greater than John the Baptist; yet the least in the Kingdom of Heaven is greater than he. From the days of John the Baptist until now, the Kingdom of Heaven suffers violence, and the*

---

[108] This story of John the Baptist's death is also mentioned by Flavius Josephus, cf *Antiquities* 18.5.2 paragraph 118. Herod Antipas, the son of Herod the Great, arrested John because he publically condemned his marriage to his brother's wife, which was forbidden by Moses as long as the wife's husband was still alive. Herod imprisoned John at Machaerus, a mountain fortress located on the eastern side of the Dead Sea near the Jordan River. Josephus' account makes no mention of Herod's daughter nor of bringing the head of John the Baptist to Herod's wife Herodias, implying that this may have added by Mark, who is the original source. Perhaps he embellished the story to degrade the reader's opinion of Herod and his wife since Herod was guilty of many evil acts.

*violent are taking it by force. All the prophets and the law prophesied up to the time of John. And, if you are willing to accept it, he is Elijah, the one who is to come.*[109] *Whoever has ears ought to hear."*[110]

(Matt 11:7-15)

Then he left the crowds and went off by himself to a deserted place. However, the crowds would not leave him alone and they soon went to the place where he had gone.

*"When… he saw the vast crowd, his heart was moved with pity for them, and he cured their sick.*

*When it was evening, the disciples approached him and said, "This is a deserted place, and it is already late: dismiss the crowds so that they can go to the villages and buy food for*

---

[109]  There was a common belief that either Elijah or a prophet like Elijah would appear before the Messiah. When Matthew's Jesus says that John is Elijah, he is subtly saying he is the Messiah

[110]  John the Baptist had a very large number of followers since the gospels tell us that everyone from Judea and Jerusalem and the whole area around the Jordan came to him to be baptized, cf Matt 4:5-6. No doubt this is an exaggeration but still it tells us John had many followers. Flavius Josephus gives John more press than Jesus. Evidence in Acts 19:1-7 tells us followers of John the Baptist were encountered by Paul in Ephesus in the 50's A.D. Acts 18:24-25 tells us a man named Apollos came to Corinth in the 50's A.D. from Alexandra knowing only about the baptism of John. Both the Gospels of Luke and John imply that the Baptist's movement was alive and well at the end of the first century and into the second. Some even believed John was the Messiah instead of Jesus. This was promoted by the common belief that the greater would baptize a subordinate, not the other way around.

*themselves." [Jesus} said to them, "There is no need for them
to go away; give them some food yourselves."*

*But they said to him, "Five loaves and two fish are all we have
here" Then he said, "Bring them here to me," And he ordered
the crowd to sit down on the grass. Taking the five loaves and
the two fish, and looking up the heaven, he said the blessing,
broke the loaves and gave them to the disciples, who gave them
to the crowds. They all ate and were satisfied, and they picked
up the fragments left over- the twelve wicker baskets full.*[111]

(Matt 14: 14-21*)*

"What just happened?" I asked myself. Yeshua only had five
barely loaves and a couple of fish and now we have twelve baskets
of leftovers! Was I hypno- tized? Did I fall asleep? People took what
they needed and passed on what remained and everyone ate their
fill and we had so much more than we started with. Moses fed the
Exiles in the desert with manna; Elijah fed a hundred men with
twenty barely loaves but Yeshua just fed thousands with just a few
loaves. How? Who is this Man?

---

[111] The miracle of the loaves and fishes is the only miracle found in all four
Gospels. Matthew and Mark add another miraculous feeding of the 4000.
These miracles prefigure the great Messianic banquet that was expected
when the Messiah established his kingdom. The story has Eucharistic
overtones, especially in John's version where Jesus himself distributes the
Bread. It also looks back to when the Israelites were fed with manna in the
desert, cf Ex 16 and when Elijah fed a hundred men with only twenty loaves
and some grain, cf 2 Kings 4:42-44. In light of this, the story is revealing
a theme common to all four gospels- that Jesus is greater than Moses and
Elijah. The twelve baskets of leftovers obviously symbolize the twelve tribes
of Israel perhaps symbolizing that no one will be left unfed in the Kingdom
which is to come.

Once we realized what he had done we all stood up praising Hashem. But some cried out, "He is the Prophet;"[112] others said, "He is the Messiah." Yudah Iscariot began running through the crowd crying out, "Yeshua our King! Yeshua our King!" Yeshua, realizing what was happening, slipped away into the hills before they could seize him.

---

[112] There was a traditional belief that a Prophet like Moses would arise in Israel and establish a new Kingdom.

## Chapter Nine

～

# The return to Bethany

After the crowds were dispersed, Cephas, Yacob, Andreas and I went to look for him. When we found him he said, "We must leave this place for a while or else the crowds will try to force me to be their king, especially with Yudah trying to stir them up. Let us go to Bethany, Eleazar."

We joined a caravan where we could be protected from robbers and Yeshua could easily hide himself for most were travelers from afar eager to sell their wares in Jerusalem and Alexandria. Along the way Jesus continued to teach us.

*"Stop judging and you will not be judged. Stop condemning and you will not be condemned. Forgive and you will be forgiven. Give and gifts will be given you; a good measure, packed together, shaken down and overflowing, will be poured in your lap. For the measure with which you measure will in return be measured out to you." And he told them a parable, "Can a blind person guide a blind person? "Will not both fall into a pit? No disciple is superior to the teacher; but, when fully trained, every disciple will be like his teacher. Why do you notice the splinter in your brother's eye but do not perceive*

*the wooden beam in your own? You hypocrite! Remove the*
*beam from your own eye first; then you will see clearly the*
*splinter in your brother's eye.*" [113]

(Lk 6:37- 42)

I had heard these words before when he spoke them to my sisters and me at our house. But this time I felt ashamed. I had judged the twelve harshly. I told myself I was superior to them because I was educated and wealthy. I had belittled them and called them illiterate peasants, crude Galileans, hot tempered buffoons. I fell to my knees and cried out, "Forgive me Lord for I am guilty of these sins and do not deserve to be a disciple" He smiled and looked at me will love, "Believe me when I say this Eleazar; you are not far from the Kingdom of Hashem. Know that you are forgiven and allow Hashem to mold you and truly shape you into his image." [114] Then he turned to the others and said,

---

[113] Luke's version of Matt 7:1-5. Judging others is perhaps our most common sin. Often we condemn others for the same faults we have. That's why Jesus calls us hypocrites. This is one of the few times he calls someone other than the Scribes and Pharisees hypocrites so we know this is a very serious subject. Worse than the sin is our punishment which will be harsh. If we dare to call ourselves Christians we must stop judging others and learn to forgive others.

[114] Food for thought. Adam and Eve were said to have been created in God's image. After they sinned were they no longer in God's image? Surely it was tarnished. Paul believed Jesus was the new Adam. Whereas Adam sinned Jesus did not, whereas Adam and Eve were disobedient, Jesus was obedient even unto death, cf Phil 2:8. Because of this, Paul tells us in Rom 8:29 that we are the firstborn of many brothers. Through baptism we are reborn and become new persons in Christ, cf 2 Cor 5:17. Consequently, because of Jesus death on the cross we become like the first Adam before he sinned and therefor destined for everlasting life.

*A good tree does not bear rotten fruit nor does a rotten tree*
*bear good fruit. For every tree is known by its own fruit.*
*For people do not pick figs from thorn bushes, nor do they*
*gather grapes from brambles. A good person out of the store of*
*goodness in his heart produces good, but an evil person out of*
*the store of evil produces evil; for from the fullness of the heart*
*the mouth speaks.* "[115]

(Lk 6:43-45)

When we arrived at my home in Bethany my servant Phanuel
greeted us and led us out to the courtyard. My father had many
servants,[116] most of whom I gave their freedom. When my sisters
heard Yeshua had come to visit they were so excited. Martha
immediately went to the kitchen to prepare a meal for us assisted
by her maid servant Aria. My sister Miriam wished to stay with
us. When we objected that it was not proper for her to be among
men, Yeshua insisted she stay. He looked at each of us, one at a
time and said:

*Whoever receives you receives me and whoever receives me*
*receives the one who sent me. Whoever receives a prophet*
*because he is a prophet, will receive a prophet's reward and*

---

[115]  The fundamental teaching here is good begets good and evil begets evil.
The true disciple abhors evil and anything that leads to evil. Therefore, his
heart is pure and a pure heart produces good fruit.

[116]  Servants or slaves were common throughout the Roman Empire. In
Israel, they could be Jewish or foreign. Jewish slaves to some extent were
protected by the Law of Moses. Like the Jews, they could not work on
the Sabbath and they could not be killed. Many became an integral part
of the household and even participated in the Passover celebration. Some
female slaves married their owners, upon which they immediately became
free. Owners could give their slaves freedom any time they wished.

*whoever receives a righteous man because he is righteous will receive a righteous man's reward. And whoever gives only a cup of cold water to one of these little ones to drink because he is a disciple- amen, I say to you, he will surely not lose his reward.*[117]

(Matt 10:40-43)

While Yeshua was speaking, Phanuel announced we had visitors. A few of my father's friends who were Pharisees entered the room. After my father died , they would occasionally come to reminisce and ask how we were doing. They were good friends but they avoided Miriam because of her past. They were surprised to see Yeshua for they certainly knew him from the days he spent teaching in the Temple. We were about to eat and I invited them to sit at table with us. They sat but only drank wine. We were famished because of our long journey so after Yeshua said the blessing we immediately started to eat.

They said to Yeshua, "Why do your disciples break the tradition of the elders but instead eat a meal with unclean hands?"

He responded, "Well did Isaiah prophesy about you hypocrites, as it is written:

'*This people honors me with their lips,
but their hearts are far from me;
In vain do they worship me,
teaching as doctrines human precepts*'[118]

---

[117] A prophet is one who speaks for God. Prophets were deemed a ministry in the early Church. St. Paul, in 1Corinthians 14 describes the role of prophecy and its importance. Verse 42 is reminiscent of Matt 25:35, *I was thirsty and you gave me to drink* and Matt 25:40, *whatever you did for one these least brothers of mine you did it for me.*

[118] The Pharisees were notorious for adding rules to the Law of Moses, especially where Moses did not specifically define a law or rule. So they had many man made laws.

*You disregard God's commandment but you cling to human tradition." He went on to say, "How well you have set aside the commandment of God in order to uphold your tradition! For Moses said, 'Honor your father and your mother, and whoever curses his father or mother shall die. ' Yet, you say, 'If a person says to father or mother, "Any support you might have had from me is* **qorban**" ' *(meaning dedicated to God),*[119] *you allow him to do nothing more for his father or mother. You nullify the word of God in favor of your tradition that you handed on. And you do many such things." *[120]

(Mk 7:5 - 13)

My friends, obviously upset, got up abruptly, excused themselves and left. I was upset as well and I asked Yeshua why he had embarrassed them. He said to me, "Eleazar, your friends, like your father, are good and holy men who are more faithful to the Law than many others but their hearts are in the wrong place. They have become so absorbed with external things they forget why the law was given to them. The law is not about ritual; it is about love. There is nothing bad about washing one's hands before one eats but to make it a rule for all is not about love; for the poor cannot wash their hands. They do not have the bowls or even the water to do so. Are they then defiled and condemned by my Father? Of course not, for my Father loves the

---

[119] *Qorban* was a formula whereby one could make a financial offering to the Temple which absolved them from using this money to care for one's parents.

[120] This text is basically a polemic against the distorting power of legalism.

poor as well as the rich, the unrighteous as well as the righteous. We must not make rules which separate us. Rather, we must love as my Father loves so that we can unite ourselves to all people." He turned to the other disciples and said what he said to me on the road to Jerusalem,

*"Nothing that enters from the outside can defile that person; but the things that come out from within are what defile."*

(Mk 7:15)

The next morning, before we returned to Capernaum, we decided to go to Jerusalem and make an offering to the Temple. We arrived early in the morning and as we were exiting the Temple into the courtyard some of the Scribes and Pharisees came to Yeshua dragging a woman by her hair and threw her down at his feet. They said to him:

*"Teacher, this woman was caught in the very act of committing adultery. Now, in the law, Moses commanded us to stone such a woman. So, what do you say? They said this to test him, so that they could have some charge to bring against him. Jesus bent down and began to write on the ground with his finger. But, when they continued asking him, he straightened up and said to them, "Let the one who is without sin be the first to throw a stone at her." Again he bent down and wrote on the ground. And in response , they went away one by one, beginning with the elders. So, he was left alone with the woman before him. Then Jesus straightened up and said to her, "Woman, where are they? Has no one condemned you?" She replied, "No one sir." Jesus*

*said, "Neither do I condemn you. Go, [and] from now on do not sin anymore."*[121]

(Jn 8:4-11)

When I saw the woman lying there I could only think of Miriam. She had been betrothed but her betrothed took advantage of her before the wedding and then, when found out, cast her off, saying she seduced him. My sister pleaded with my father saying she did not have the authority to stop it, for a man, in this case, was rarely, if ever, deemed to be at fault. My Father, although a staunch Pharisee pitied her, paid off her betrothed, and allowed her to stay in our home. Still, her reputation was now known and she would never be able to marry or have children because she was seen as defiled. It was only now that I understood how she must have felt. I must tell her what Yeshua did today for she will know that in his eyes she is not defiled; only loved.

---

[121]  This story is not in older Protestant Bibles because it is not found in the oldest Greek manuscripts containing the Gospel of John. It is only found in later Latin texts. It is also found in one of the manuscripts containing the Gospel of Luke and, in fact, the text sounds more like Luke than John. It was likely inserted in John's Gospel late in the second century but it is still considered canonical by the Catholic Church. The story obviously exemplifies Jesus' command not to judge others and like so many other passages contradicts the law of Moses. According to Leviticus 20:10 the penalty for adultery was taking both the man and the woman to the city gate and stoning them to death. The injustice in this case is immediately seen by Jesus since the other party is not there. He also knows they can't stone her away from the gate since that would not be in accordance with the law of Moses. They tried to trap Jesus but Jesus' response was brilliant wherein he not only found a way out of the trap but also used the occasion to demonstrate that we are not to judge and mercy can supersede the law.

## Chapter Ten

~~~

# More challenges in Capernaum

When we reached Capernaum, to keep away from the crowds, we immediately got into Andreas' and Cephas' boat and sailed across Lake Galilee to the Gentile territory of the Gerasenes[122].

*When he came ashore a man from the town who was possessed by demons met him. For a long time he had not worn clothes; he did not live in a house, but lived among the tombs. When he saw Jesus he cried out and fell down before him; in a loud voice he shouted, "What have you to do with me, Jesus, son of the Most High God? I beg you, do not torment me." For he had ordered the unclean spirit to come out of the man. It had taken hold of him many times and he used to be bound with chains and shackles as a restraint, but he would break his bonds and be driven by the demon into deserted places. Then Jesus said to him, "What is your name?" He replied, "Legion,"[123] because*

---

[122] Probably a part of the Decapolis mentioned earlier.

[123] There was a popular belief that knowing a spirit's name gave you authority over it. When Moses asked for God's name at the burning bush, notice He did not give him His name. He simply said, "I am who am".

*many demons had entered him.*[124] *And they pleaded with him not to order them to depart into the abyss.*

*A herd of many swine was feeding there on the hillside, and they pleaded with him to allow them to enter the swine; and he let them.*[125] *The demons came out of the man and entered the swine, and the herd rushed down the steep bank into the water and was drowned.*[126] *When the swine herders saw what had happened, they ran away and reported the incident in the town and throughout the countryside. People came out to see what had happened and, when they approached Jesus, they discovered the man from whom the demons had come out sitting at his feet.*[127] *He was clothed and in his right mind, and they were seized with fear. Those who witnessed it told them how the possessed man had been saved. The entire population in the region of the Gerasenes asked Jesus to leave*

---

[124] A Roman legion is about 5000 men.

[125] The presence of a herd of pigs confirms they are in Gentile territory since pigs would not be raised in Israel because they were an unclean animal.

[126] The ancients believe water was both sacred and profane. Ritual ablutions cleansed one who was deemed unclean. John's baptism allowed for a fresh moral start. However, large bodies of water were deemed to house evil spirits including the infamous Leviathan mentioned in the Old Testament. Notice it's called the abyss, the description of the chaotic universe before the creation. They were literally trapped there. To drown at sea was the worst thing that could happen because figuratively, if not actually, one was being immersed in a cauldron of evil. So the symbolism is clear. When the pigs drowned, the demons would be trapped in the waters forever and therefore could not escape to harm anyone else. They had asked not to be driven into the abyss but ironically ended there anyway.

[127] Notice than man has taken the position of a disciple sitting before his master.

*because they were seized with great fear.* [128]*So he got into the boat and returned.*

(Lk 8:27-35)

When we sailed back to Capernaum no one spoke. We really didn't know what to say. Watching Yeshua drive out demons was unnerving. This time it was frightening. There were so many screaming and screeching at him. They claimed to know who he was. They called him son of the Most High God. What did they mean? Then watching Jesus was frightful. His face would become contorted, saliva would come out of his mouth; he would begin to shake- today it was violently, probably because there were so many demons. Then, when they were finally expelled, Yeshua was so exhausted he could hardly move. He just sat down and quietly comforted the man who was dazed, barely realizing what had happened.

Why did the demons call him the son of the Most High God? What did they know that we didn't?

When we reached Capernaum we were joined by the rest of the twelve and surprisingly some women. Apparently, when I wasn't with him he cured them of their infirmities and they chose to follow him. This was deemed inappropriate by all of us for women usually traveled separately, even from their husbands. These women kept to themselves but still the scribes and the Pharisees and others will find this behavior unacceptable.

The names of the women were: Miriam from Magdala from whom Yeshua drove out seven demons, Suzanna and Yohanna, the wife of Herod's steward Chuza. There were other women as well and most were wealthy and provided for all of us out of their

---

[128]  They had lost a whole herd. They didn't want Jesus to do any more damage to their economy!

resources, so most of the Twelve did not complain about their being among us. I too provided money for food but I asked Yeshua not to say anything about it to the others.[129]

We went into the synagogue and a scribe stood up to test him and said,

> *"Teacher,*[130] *what must I do to inherit eternal life?" Jesus said to him, "What is written in the law? How do you read it?" He said in reply, "You shall love the Lord your God with all your heart, with all your being, with all your strength and with all your mind and your neighbor as yourself."*[131] *He replied to him, "You have answered correctly; do this and you shall live."*

> *But, because he wished to justify himself, he said to Jesus, "And who is my neighbor?" Jesus replied, "A man fell victim to robbers as he went down from Jerusalem to Jericho. They stripped and beat him and went off leaving him half dead. A priest happened to be going down that road, but when he saw him, he passed by on the other side. Likewise a Levite*[132] *came to the place, and when he saw him, he passed by on the*

---

[129] For details cf Lk 8:1-3. There is no record that Lazarus donated money to the cause but, since he was wealthy and was very close to Jesus, it is likely he did.

[130] Teacher is one of the translations for the word *rabbi*. It can also be translated as *master*.

[131] This is part of a confessional statement found in Deuteronomy 6:5-9. It begins with the words, "Hear oh Israel, Adonai our God is one, Adonai is our God." It is then followed by the two great commandments mentioned here. Devout Jews prayed this prayer, called the Schema, three times a day.

[132] Levites were subordinate to Temple officials and never obtained the full priesthood and, as such, were considered lower clergy who did menial tasks in the Temple. Similar to a Permanent Deacon!

*opposite side. But a Samaritan traveler who came upon him was moved with compassion at the sight. He approached the victim, poured oil and wine over his wounds and bandaged them. Then he lifted him up on his own animal, took him to an inn and cared for him. The next day he took out two silver coins and gave them to the innkeeper with the instruction, 'Take care of him. If you spend more than what I have given you, I shall repay you on my way back. Which of these three, in your opinion, was neighbor to the robbers' victim?" He answered, "The one who treated him with mercy." Jesus said to him, "Go and do likewise."*[133]

(Lk10:25-37)

After this we left the synagogue, and summoning the twelve he,

*…gave them power and authority over all demons and to cure diseases,*[134] *and he sent them to proclaim the Kingdom*

---

[133] The Good Samaritan is one the most well-known of Jesus' parables. It demonstrates Jesus' common theme that love and/or mercy always trumps legalism. Notice that the *neighbor* is a Samaritan who is an enemy of the Jews and vice versa. The priest and Levite, two people who certainly know the meaning of the law to love one's neighbor, pass him by. Since they passed him on the other side of the road they may have been going to the Temple to offer sacrifice. If the victim was dead or bleeding and they touched him they would be ritually unclean and unable to serve in the temple until they had bathed for several days. As a result, they would lose their turn to serve in the temple which was a great honor. This lesson echoes the words of Jesus when he says in Matthew 9:13, "I desire mercy not sacrifice".

[134] This episode is reflected in Acts after the descent of the Holy Spirit on Pentecost. In Acts 2:8 Jesus tells the disciples that they "will receive power when the Holy Spirit comes. Before that they were cowards hiding from the authorities. They did not preach or work any miracles. Their clothing and disposition resembles Paul's missionary journeys and descriptions

*of God and to heal [the sick]. He said to them, "Take no walking stick, nor sack nor food nor money, and let no one take a second tunic. Whatever house you enter, stay there and leave from there. And as for those who do not welcome you, when you leave that town, shake the dust from your feet in testimony against them. Then they set out and went from village to village proclaiming the good news and curing diseases everywhere.*

(Lk 9:1-6)

---

of evangelists and prophets as described in the Didache, a first century Christian catechism. So, the instructions given by Jesus in this section of Luke (as well as Matthew and Mark) are probably instructions given to the Apostles by the risen Lord Jesus through Christian Prophets. As you shall see later, the Transfiguration is likely a post-resurrection event as well.

This is not uncommon, especially in the later gospels. Paul makes it very clear that he had ongoing conversations with the risen Christ who guided his decision-making and taught him his theology. As I mentioned above, I believe the Gospel of John contains mostly the words of the risen Lord Jesus rather than Jesus in the flesh.

## CHAPTER ELEVEN

# Proclaiming the gospel to the Gentiles

Shortly after the Twelve returned from their missionary work we went on a two day journey to Tyre, a Gentile town on the coast of the Great Sea. Yeshua was concerned about Herod and the Temple priests who had sent messengers to spy on us.[135] When we came near the city we were immediately approached by a Canaanite woman who called out,

*"Have pity on me, Lord, Son of David! My daughter is tormented by a demon."* [136]*But he did not say a word to answer her. His disciples came and said to him, "Send her*

---

[135] Close examination of Jesus' itinerary in Galilee indicates he stayed near the northern borders of the province which meant he could easily escape into Gentile territory and away from Herod's clutches. It is only after Peter's confession in Caesarea Philipp, the northern most towns in Galilee that Jesus journeys through Galilee on his way back to Jerusalem.

[136] Notice that she, although a Gentile, seems to know who he is. Also, notice how she "came and did him homage", echoing the words used when the Magi, also Gentiles, entered the house in Bethlehem, cf Matt 2:11.

*away, for she keeps calling out after us." He said in reply,*
*"I was sent only to the lost sheep of the house of Israel." But*
*the woman came and did him homage, saying, "Lord, help*
*me." He said in reply, "It is not right to take the food of the*
*children and throw it to the dogs." [137] She said, "Please Lord,*
*for even the dogs eat the scraps that fall from the table of their*
*masters." Then Jesus said in reply, "O woman, great is your*
*faith! Let it be done for you as you wish." And her daughter*
*was healed at that hour [138]*

(Matt 15:21-28)

We were surprised to learn that Yeshua was known even among
the Gentiles in Syria. So, we left Tyre and traveled further into
Syria to the city of Sidon.[139] We stayed there for several days and
after Jesus was well rested we made our way back to Lake Galilee
into the district of the Decapolis.[140] But it wasn't long before they
found out he had returned. We were surprised by their welcome
since the last time we were there Jesus had sent demons into a
herd of pigs that ran into Lake Galilee and drowned. They were
so frightened and concerned they had asked us to leave.

*And people brought him a deaf man who had a speech*
*impediment and begged him to lay his hand on him. He took*
*him off by himself, away from the crowd. He put his finger into*

---

[137] The words dogs and swine were commonly used by the Jews in reference to
the Gentiles. Jesus' use here seems unusually harsh coming from him as he
is portrayed as being very tolerant to everyone except the leaders of the Jews.

[138] We see again that faith brings healing and salvation. Soon we will see how
her strong faith is contrasted with the weak faith of the disciples.

[139] Sidon was a major seaport for the ancient Phoenicians. Presently, it is located
in Lebanon.

[140] Notice again how Jesus continues to remain outside the jurisdiction of Herod.

*the man's ears and spitting,*[141] *touched his tongue; then he looked up to heaven and groaned, and said to him, "Ephpatha!" (That is, "Be opened") And, immediately], the man's ears were opened and he spoke plainly. He ordered them not to tell anyone. But the more he ordered them not to, the more they proclaimed it.*[142]

(Mk 7:31-36)

Because of the crowds, we left that place and went to Bethsaida, the small fishing village on the north shore of Lake Galilee where Cephas and Andreas lived.[143]

*When they arrived at Bethsaida, they brought a blind man and begged him to touch him. He took the blind man by the hand and led him outside the village. Putting spittle*[144] *on his eyes he laid his hands on him and asked, "Do you see anything?" Looking up he said, "I see people looking like trees and walking. Then he laid his hands on his eyes a second time and he saw clearly; his sight was restored and he could see everything distinctly. Then he sent him home and said, "Do not even go into the village."*[145]

(Mk 8:22-26)

---

[141] The use of spittle here may have a sacramental quality- the use of a material substance as a sign of grace. It's the first time we see Jesus heal using something other than his word or touch.

[142] Another example of the Messianic Secret mentioned above.

[143] John 1:44 & 12:21 says that Bethsaida was the home of Peter and his brother Andrew instead of Capernaum. Phillip was also from this town.

[144] This is the second instance of Jesus using spittle as an agent for healing. In John 9:6 Jesus makes clay using his saliva when he heals the man who was born blind.

[145] The word for *see* in Greek can also imply faith. Most likely, this story is allegorical. The fact that the man sees gradually indicates that often faith starts out gradually and intensifies the more open we are to the gospel.

# CHAPTER TWELVE

# The kingdom and its Messiah

Again, because of the crowds we left and set out for the villages of Caesarea Philippi.[146]

*Along the way, Jesus asked his disciples, "Who do people say that I am?"[147] They said in reply, "John the Baptist, others Elijah, still others one of the prophets." And he asked them, "But who do you say that I am?" Peter said to him in reply,*

---

[146] Caesarea Philippi is a group of the northern most towns in Galilee located near the source of the Jordan River. It was rebuilt by Philip who was tetrarch of Iturea, also called Bashan and area originally assigned to the tribe of Manasseh, cf Josh 13:8-33.

[147] There was a common belief among the Jews that the agreement of two or more people was required to validate the truth of one's testimony. I believe, along with many other scholars, that Jesus did not know who he was in the beginning of his ministry. At this point in Mark's Gospel, which marks the turning point, Jesus has become aware of his identity and is simply asking the disciples for validation.

*"You are the Messiah."*[148] *Then he warned them not to tell anyone about him.*[149]

(Mk 8:27-30).

This is not the first time I have been dumbstruck by something Yeshua did or said and I'm sure it won't be the last. We all were excited expecting to be a part of the army Yeshua was going to gather up to conquer the Romans. I was even thinking how I would help him rule his kingdom. Then he literally destroyed those dreams in an instant.

*He began to teach them that the Son of Man*[150] *must suffer greatly and be rejected by the elders, the chief priests and the*

---

[148] Peter is always first among those listed as apostles. Also, as I stated above, along with James and John, he was said to be privy to special events, like the raising of Jairus' Daughter and the Transfiguration. It probably was not that way in the beginning. He was not the head of the Jerusalem Church. It appears that James and his brother John were seen as superior to Peter until James was martyred in 44 A.D. After that, James, known as the brother of Jesus, became the outright leader of the Brethren in Jerusalem. Shortly after about 50 A.D. Galatians 2:9 tells us that Peter left Jerusalem and preached the gospel to the Jews. Still, Paul calls him one of the "Pillars" but I think he really became a real force in the Church after the middle of the first century and this was reflected in the gospel stories, all of which were written after Peter died.

[149] In Matthew's version of this story Jesus says to Peter, "flesh and blood has not revealed this to you, but my heavenly Father," cf Matt 16:17, indicating what he said was via the inspiration of the Holy Spirit.

[150] Son of Man is an enigmatic title used in Daniel 7:13-14. However, the gospels use this phrase in two different ways. The most common is *bar nasha* which simply means an ordinary human being. God addresses Ezekiel this way ninety times However, during his trial, Jesus responds to the High Priest with the words, "...and you will see the Son of Man seated at the right hand of the Power and coming on the clouds of heaven," (Mk 14:62).

*scribes, and be killed, and rise after three days. He spoke this openly. Then Peter took him aside and began to rebuke him. At this he turned around and, looking at his disciples, rebuked Peter and said, "Get behind me you Satan.*[151] *You are thinking not as God does, but as human beings do."*

(Mk 8:31-33)

I never saw Yeshua so angry. I can't believe he called Cephas a Satan.[152] Cephas was like a chastised puppy, his face fell, and his shoulders slumped. Tears welled up in his eyes and he couldn't speak. Yet, like Cephas, none of us could believe Jesus was going to be killed. How could he usher in his kingdom if he were dead? We surely misunderstood him. Why does he still speak in riddles?

*A crowd had now gathered and Jesus turned and said to them, "Whoever wishes to come after me must deny himself, take up his cross, and follow me. For whoever wishes to save his life will lose it, but whoever loses his life for my sake and that of the gospel will save it. What profit is there for one to gain the whole world and forfeit his life? What could one give in exchange for his life? Whoever is ashamed of me and of my words in this faithless and sinful generation, the Son of Man*

---

This is an allusion to Daniel 7:14 that refers to a "Son of Man" appearing at the end of the world and who will have dominion over an everlasting kingdom. So, in this sense Jesus is revealing to the High Priest that he is the long awaited Messiah. It still begs the question of why Jesus repeatedly refers to himself as a mere man.

[151] Satan pronounced "say tane" in Hebrew is not personified in Old Testament Judaism but rather refers to a temptation or a difficulty to overcome. This is the meaning of Jesus' use of it here in reference to Peter.

[152] Satan can also mean *adversary*. In the O.T. he can be an ordinary human being or a divine emissary. In the N.T. it is synonymous with a devil or *the* devil.

*will be ashamed of when he comes in his Father's glory with the holy angels.*[153]

(Mk 8:34-38)

"Now that's more like it," said Yudah. "He's back to talking about coming in glory with his angels. Of course we'll make sacrifices. We'll deny everything because the reward will be power and glory and we will reign with him sitting on the twelve thrones that surround our king!"

Yeshua shook his head slowly and looked at Yudah with a terrible sadness in his gaze. Yudah did not see him. I wondered what it meant. There was so much I didn't understand. As far as material possessions were concerned, I had gained the whole world. I had not lost my life. And, if I sold it all I would gain my life? How? He continues to bewilder me.

After this we traveled back to Capernaum. Yeshua was no longer afraid to be out with the crowds. He no longer warned people to keep his miracles a secret. He was on a mission that would take him back to Jerusalem. When we reached Capernaum, Miriam, the mother of Yacob and Yohanan, approached him with her sons and a request:

---

[153] Chapter 8 is often called the turning point in Mark's gospel. Up till now it's basically been about miracles, the kingdom and keeping Jesus' identity secret. Now the cat is out of the bag so to speak. Both he and the disciples know he is the Messiah. So, for the rest of the gospel, Jesus will focus on the meaning of his messiahship and a fuller meaning of the kingdom. They are not what they think. Both are about sacrifice, penance and denial; about suffering for the sake of the gospel and ultimately his suffering on the cross. The sad part is they will not get it until after he dies and, some, like Judas, will never get it. In fact, even today, many who dare to call ourselves Christians still don't get it.

*[Jesus] said to her, "What do you wish?" She answered him, "Command that these sons of mine sit, one at your right and the other at your left, in your kingdom." Jesus said in reply, "You do not know what you are asking. Can you drink the cup* **that I am going to drink?" They said to him, "We can."** *He replied, "My cup you will indeed drink, but to sit at my right and at my left, [this] is not mine to give but is for those for whom it has been prepared by my Father." When the [others] heard this they became indignant at the two brothers. But Jesus summoned them and said, "You know that the rulers of the Gentiles lord it over them, and the great ones make their authority over them felt. But it shall not be so among you. Rather, whoever wishes to be great among you shall be your servant; whoever wishes to be first among you shall be your slave. Just so, the Son of Man did not come to be served but to serve and to give his life as a ransom for many."*[154]

(Matt 20:21-28)

Yeshua stopped walking for a moment but continued to teach us:

---

[154] Matthew is showing his readers how the disciples didn't understand Jesus' mission or the meaning of his kingdom. To them it was temporal, like the previous Jewish kingdoms. After the admission that he is the Messiah, Jesus will spend the rest of his time on earth trying to make them understand that his kingdom is very different than worldly kingdoms, most notably by the service of its leaders. The word *cup* here symbolizes martyrdom. It's interesting that both John and James apparently die a martyr's death. James was martyred in 44 A.D. but legend says John lived to the end of the first century and wrote his gospel. Some scholars insist that this passage indicates Matthew and Mark know this is not the case. Since they were written before The Gospel of John they imply John died well before the gospel that credits him as the evangelist. This supports my argument that John is not the Beloved Disciple.

*"If any one wishes to be first, he shall be the last of all and the servant of all." Taking a child he placed it in their midst, and putting his arms around it said to them, "Whoever receives one child such as this in my name, receives me; and whoever receives me, receives not me but the one who sent me."*[155]

(Mk 9:35-37)

I'm beginning to get an idea of what Yeshua's kingdom is about. It's not like the kingdoms of the world. That's becoming obvious. It's more like the reverse of those kingdoms. It's a kingdom that may not be gained by waging war or winning battles. It's something that will start out very small like the mustard seed and the leaven, perhaps with only a few followers like us. It will have the value of a great treasure but it won't be a great treasure in a worldly way. And then, if we successfully established this kingdom we won't be sitting on thrones and lording over others; rather we will be serving others. But how? Surely Yeshua will be ushering in this kingdom, but again how will he do it?

When I mentioned these thoughts to Yeshua he looked at me with love and said, "Eleazar, you are not far from the Kingdom of Hashem." I was flattered but truthfully there was so much I didn't understand.

As we left Capernaum, and began our journey through Galilee, Yeshua continued to teach us:

*"The Son of Man is to be handed over to men and they will kill him, and three days after his death he will rise." But*

---

[155]  In the first century Church the word child or children referred to the believer. John uses it once in this way as do the epistles of John. The Didache refers to those in the community as "my children" or "my child". This reference is most likely used because, like children, believers were meek and humble and had no official status.

*they did not understand the saying, and they were afraid to
question him.*

(Mk 9:31-32)

*Who is the Son of Man,* I wondered.[156] Surely it's not Yeshua.
How can he usher in the Kingdom of Hashem if he dies? And,
what does rising from the dead mean?

We now were heading to Jerusalem but we did not go by way
of Samaria. Instead, we mostly followed the west side of the Jordan
River which would eventually take us to Jericho. From there it was
less than a day's journey to Jerusalem. As we neared Mount Tabor
Yeshua took Cephas, Yacob and Yohanan off to the top of it. A few
months later Cephas shared what happened.

*Jesus was transfigured before them: His face shone like the sun
and his clothes became white as light.*[157] *And behold Moses
and Elijah appeared to them conversing with him.*[158] *Then
Peter said to Jesus in reply, "Lord, it is good that we are here!
I will make three tents: one for you, one for Moses and one
for Elijah." While he was still speaking , behold, a bright*

---

[156] Some believe that the Son of Man was someone other than Jesus but this is
highly unlikely.

[157] As I mentioned before, I believe this was a post resurrection experience
because it doesn't seem to fit before Jesus died and rose. The glorified body
of Jesus was more likely to be transfigured than his human body. Notice
the similarity between Jesus' face and Moses' face. When Moses came down
from Mt. Sinai his face was so bright he had to cover it with a cloth. This
is consistent with Matthew's depiction of Jesus as the new Moses.

[158] The presence of Moses and Elijah represent the Law and the prophets, two
of the three main parts of the Old Testament. Jesus standing between them
signifies he is superior to both. Jesus will replace the old covenant with the
new and everlasting covenant.

*cloud cast a shadow over them, then from the cloud came a voice that said, "This is my beloved Son, with whom I am well pleased; listen to him."*[159] *When the disciples heard this they fell prostrate and were very much afraid. But Jesus came and touched them, saying, "Rise and do not be afraid." And when the disciples raised their eyes, they saw no one else but Jesus alone.*

(Matt 17:1-8)

---

[159] Ex 40:34 describes a cloud coming over the meeting tent indicating the presence of God. Notice the similarity between the words spoken by God and the words spoken to Jesus at his baptism.

≈

# CHAPTER THIRTEEN

# Going up to Jerusalem

We left Mt Tabor and continued our way up to Jerusalem. On the way we stopped at Nain. By the time we reached the entrance into the city a large crowd was following us.

> *As he drew near the gate of the city, a man who had died was being carried out, the only son of his mother, and she was a widow. A large crowd from the city was with her. When the Lord saw her, he was moved with pity for her and said to her, "Do not weep." He stepped forward and touched the coffin; at this the bearers halted, and he said, "Young man, I tell you arise!" The dead man sat up and began to speak, and Jesus gave him to his mother. Fear seized all of them and they glorified God exclaiming, "A great prophet has arisen in our midst," and "God has visited his people."*[160]
>
> (Lk 7:12-16)

I find it so hard to believe the boy was really dead. How could Yeshua possibly raise someone from the dead? Yet, Cephas swears

---

[160] Elijah also raised the only son of a widow from Zarephath, cf 1 Kings 7:18-24.

that Yairus' daughter was dead. But Yeshua himself said she was only sleeping. Perhaps this boy was only sleeping. Still, they were taking him for burial. The woman was beside herself with joy. The death of her only son left her defenseless against a very cruel world. Widows basically have no rights. With her son dead she would have no rightful heir and the family name would disappear. Bringing her son back to life restored her place in society and gave back her dignity.

I thought of my sisters Martha and Miriam. What would happen to them if I died?

We left Nain and went across the Jordan to the city of Pella.[161]

*Again crowds gathered around him, and , as was his custom, he again taught them. The Pharisees approached and asked, "Is it lawful for a husband to divorce his wife? They were testing him. He said to them in reply. "What did Moses command you?" They replied, "Moses permitted him to write a bill of divorce and dismiss her." But Jesus told them, "Because of the hardness of your hearts he wrote you this commandment. But from the beginning of creation, God made them male and female. For this reason a man shall leave his father and mother [and be joined to his wife], and the two shall become one flesh. Therefore, what God has joined together, no human being must separate.[162] In the house the disciples*

---

[161] Epiphanius, a 4th century Church Father, claims the Christian community was warned by their prophets of the destruction of Jerusalem and told to go to the city of Pella. They established a large community there and it is alleged to be the site of one of the earliest Christian Churches. Pella is located in central Palestine in the Jordan Valley east of the river. It is not mentioned in the new Testament.

[162] The bill of divorce mentioned here could only be initiated by the husband and could be for the simplest of reasons. For example, he may not like her

*again questioned him about this. He said to them, "Whoever divorces his wife and marries commits adultery against her and if she divorces her husband and marries another, she commits adultery.*[163]

(Mk 10:1-12)

The teaching of Yeshua about divorce is strict. But then, he is not married so it's easy to be strict. Also, divorce is not common amongst us. Marriage is taken seriously but, of course, there are those who take advantage of the law, divorcing simply because they have found another woman more desirable than their wife. I myself need to start thinking about marriage as I am now twenty years old. Most men marry between the ages of eighteen and twenty four. Since I am very rich, many fathers have approached me offering their daughters but, at this time, I have little interest especially since I am responsible for my sisters.

Yeshua continued to teach the people and us.

---

eyes, she burned his supper or she simply no longer pleases him, cf Deut. 24:1. However, divorce was not common among the Jews since, if the reason was not something indecent, the husband had to give back his wife's dowry and often make other large payments as well. The writ of divorce was to guarantee the woman was free to marry, meaning that she was not an adulteress. In the case of proven adultery no writ was required since the punishment was death. However, among the poor, there often was little or no dowry and the woman was left with nothing. Also, since divorce was often deemed by most to be a failure of the wife, families could reject her leaving her with no way to survive. As a result, many of the poor divorcees resorted to prostitution. This is probably one of the reasons Jesus teaching about divorce is so strict.

[163] Obviously, Mark's audiences are Gentiles since Jewish women were not allowed to divorce their husbands.

*There is nothing concealed that will not be revealed, nor secret that will not be known. Therefore, whatever you have said in darkness will be heard in the light, and what you have whispered behind closed doors will be proclaimed to the housetops. I tell you my friends, do not be afraid of those who kill the body, but after that can do no more. I shall show you whom to fear. Be afraid of the one who after killing has the power to cast into Gehenna;[164] Yes, I tell you, be afraid of that one. Are not five small sparrows sold for two small coins? Yet, not one of them has escaped the notice of God. Even the hairs on your head have been counted. Do not be* **afraid. You are worth more than many sparrows.** *I tell you, anyone who acknowledges me before others the Son of Man will acknowledge before the angels of God. But whoever denies me will be denied before the angels of God.[165]*

(Lk 12:2-9)

Yeshua looked directly at the twelve when he said this. This was the first time I was glad I was not one of them. The burden he was laying on them was great and, while they did not understand it at the time, the tone of his voice was foreboding. Only later, after Yeshua's hour had come and gone, would we understand the meaning of his teachings.

---

[164] Gehenna was a garbage dump in Jerusalem with a sordid history. During the time of Abraham, pagans sacrificed their children to the gods in Gehenna so it was considered a place of suffering and evil. Hence, it was used by Jesus as an image for hell.

[165] The basic meaning of this parable is that one must proclaim the gospel no matter the consequences. There is no need to be afraid, even in times of suffering, because we are very important to God. Proclamation of the gospel protects us against evil. We'll only suffer the consequences of evil if we deny Christ.

We left Pella and traveled to Jericho.[166] As we entered the city we merely were going to pass through because the crowds were so large. However, there was a man sitting in a sycamore tree crying out to Yeshua. He had climbed the tree because he was short and could not see Yeshua because of the crowd.

*When he reached the place, Jesus looked up and said to him, "Zacchaeus, come down quickly, for today I must stay at your house."*

(Lk 19:5)

Stay at his house? Yeshua never said anything about staying at someone's house. Plus, after he had said this many in the crowd began booing and hissing. Obviously, this Zacchaeus was not well liked and then I wondered how Yeshua knew his name. This was the first time we had ever been in Jericho. Perhaps he was an old friend.

*And he came down quickly and received him with joy. When they all saw this, they began to grumble, saying, "He has gone to stay in the house of a sinner," [for Zacchaeus was a tax collector and also a wealthy man]. But Zacchaeus stood there and said to Jesus, "Behold, half my possessions, Lord, I shall give to the poor, and if I have extorted anything from anyone I shall repay it four times over." And Jesus said to him, "Today salvation has come to this house because this man too is a*

---

[166] Jericho, deemed the oldest known city in the world, dates back to 9000 B.C. It was the first major city conquered by Joshua and the Jews when they invaded the land of Canaan around 1100 B.C. Supposedly, its famous walls came tumbling down at the blast of a trumpet, cf Josh. 6:1-5.

*descendent of Abraham. For the Son of Man has come to seek and save the lost.* "[167]

(Lk 19 6, 2, 7-10)

Zacchaeus was a chief tax collector, the worst kind of sinner. No wonder the crowd was upset. How did Yeshua know his name? I noticed he only gave half his possessions to the poor and he was saved. Why did Yeshua ask me to give everything I had to the poor? Perhaps I could give half of my possessions. Martha and Miriam would have more than enough to live on. Still, half seems like an awful lot to give away…

We all went into Zacchaeus' home, which was even larger than mine and he served us a banquet of food. We had been living on dried fish and unleavened bread so we were grateful as we gobbled down our food. There were other tax collectors eating with us as well as some of the city's less reputable people.

*The Pharisees and scribes began to complain saying, "This man welcomes sinners and eats with them." So to them he addressed this parable, "What man among you having a hundred sheep and losing one of them would not leave the ninety-nine in the desert and go after the lost one until he finds it? And when he does find it, he sets it on his shoulders with great joy and, upon his arrival home, he calls together his friends and neighbors and says to them, 'Rejoice with me because I have found my lost sheep.' I tell you, in just the same way there will be more joy in heaven over one sinner who*

---

[167] The key to Zacchaeus' redemption is his attitude toward wealth. Without being asked, he promises to give half his possessions to the poor. In Matt 6:24 Jesus says you cannot be attached to both God and mammon. Zacchaeus demonstrated that God came first which, for Jesus, is what really matters.

*repents than over the ninety nine righteous people who have no need of repentance."*

(Lk 15:1-7)

Yeshua insisted on telling them another parable to show them the fullness of Hashem's mercy.[168]

*Then he said, "A man had two sons, and the younger son said to his father, 'Father, give me the share of the estate that should come to me. So the father divided the property between them. After a few days, the younger son collected all his belongings and set off to a distant country where he squandered his inheritance on a life of dissipation. When he had freely spent everything, a severe famine struck that country and he found himself in dire need. So he hired himself out to one of the local citizens who sent him to his farm to tend to the swine. And he longed to eat his fill of the pods on which the swine fed, but nobody gave him any. Coming to his senses he thought, 'How many of my father's hired workers have more than enough food to eat but here I am dying of hunger.[169] I shall get up and go to my father and I shall say to him, 'Father, I have sinned against heaven and against you. I no longer deserve to be called your son; treat me as one of your hired workers. So he got up and went back to his father. While he was a long way off, his father caught sight of him, and was filled with compassion.[170] He ran to his son, embraced him and*

---

[168]   The Parable of the Prodigal Son is an everyday example which explains the meaning of the parable of the lost sheep in human terms.

[169]   Feeding the swine means, as a Jew, he has reached the depths of despair.

[170]   One of the most beautiful phrases in the gospels. Notice the father has never given up on his son. He has been longing for him to come home; just as God longs for the sinner who has strayed.

*kissed him. His son said to him, 'Father, I have sinned against heaven and against you, I no longer deserve to be called your son.' But his father ordered his servants, 'Quick, bring the finest robe and put it on him; put a ring on his finger and sandals on his feet. Take the fattened calf and slaughter it.*[171] *Then let us celebrate with a feast, because this son of mine was dead and has come back to life; he was lost and has been found.'*[172] *Now, the older son had been out in the field and,* **on his way back, as he neared the house, he heard the sound of** *music and dancing. He called one of his servants and asked what this might mean. The servant said to him, 'Your brother has returned and your father has slaughtered the fattened calf because he has him back safe and sound.' He became angry and when he refused to enter the house, his father came out and pleaded with him. He said to his father in reply, 'Look,* **all these years I have served you and not once did I disobey** *your orders; yet you never gave me a young goat to feast on with my friends. But when your son returns, who swallowed up your property with prostitutes, for him you slaughtered the fattened calf.'*[173] *He said to him, 'My son, you are here* **with me always; everything I have is yours. But now we must** *celebrate and rejoice, because your brother was dead and has come back to life again; he was lost and has been found.'"*[174]

(Lk 15:11-32).

---

[171] The ring, sandals and robe are signs that he has been reinstated into the family.

[172] This is the key phrase in the story. Sin kills our souls; only God can bring us back if we are repentant.

[173] Notice the self-righteous elder son who judges rather than forgives. He wants justice. He has no love for his brother.

[174] I heard Ernest Hemmingway said this was the greatest short story ever written.

I listened to this story but could not believe it. I said to Yeshua, "The boy disgraced his father and I'm sure, made him the laughing stock of the village. What father would forgive him?

Yeshua said, "My Father."

"Yosef?" I asked.

"Not Yosef," he responded. "My father in heaven."

"Hashem?" I asked and he nodded. "But I don't understand," I said. "I know Hashem is merciful but he is also just. There was no justice here!" I could feel anger rising up within me. "The lad insulted his father and should have been punished. His name should have been stricken from the family record. His older brother should have been angry. He had been faithful all his life and his brother, who is a nothing but trash, gets rewarded. It's just not fair!"

Yeshua smiled his knowing smile and said, "Eleazar, it's not justice my Father wants, it's mercy."

"Then, there is no justice?" I asked.

Yeshua said,

*What woman having ten coins and losing one would not light a lamp and sweep the house, searching carefully until she finds it? And when she does find it, she calls together her friends and neighbors and says to them, 'Rejoice with me because I have found the coin that I lost.' In just the same way, I tell you, there will be more rejoicing among the angels [in heaven] over one sinner who repents."*

(Lk 15:8-10)

"What about the Law?" I asked. "Can we disregard the Law and still find favor with Hashem?"

Yeshua replied, "For the one who is truly repentant in his heart, all things are forgiven."

The scribes and the Pharisees were also upset by this parable. They knew they were the elder son and they knew their behavior was being judged.

In fact, they were so enraged by Yeshua's teaching they picked up stones and threw them at him. We shielded him from the stones and left Jericho immediately. He said we must hide so he decided to go to the place by the Jordan where John had baptized[175] and hide there until it was time to make his way to Jerusalem.

I had not seen my sisters for some time and I needed to check out my property and make sure all my financial responsibilities were in order. So I returned to Bethany. But, before I left, Yeshua took us aside and said,

> *"Behold, we are going up to Jerusalem, and the Son of Man will be handed over to the chief priests and the scribes, and they will condemn him to death and hand him over to the Gentiles who will mock him, spit on him, scourge him, and put him to death but after three days he will rise.*
>
> (Mk 10:31-34)

Who is this Son of Man he keeps talking about? Surely it can't be him or can it? But, if he is, how can he usher in the Kingdom of Hashem if he's dead? Surely, Hashem would not allow his Messiah to die?

---

[175] The place would be in Perea, a territory which is east of the Jordan River and just north of the Dead Sea.

# CHAPTER FOURTEEN

~~~

# Death to life

When I arrived home I did not feel well. I was feverish, weak and had difficulty breathing. My sisters were very worried and immediately sent Phanuel to find Yeshua so he could come and heal me. Later, Cephas and Martha told me what happened next.

*Now a man was ill, Lazarus from Bethany, the village of Martha and her sister Mary.[176] So the sisters sent word to him saying, 'Master, the one you love is ill.'[177] When Jesus heard this he said, "This illness is not to end in death, but is for the glory of God, that the Son of God may be glorified through it." Now Jesus loved Martha and her sister and Lazarus. So, when he heard the man was ill, he remained for two days in the place where he was.*

---

[176] I left out verse 2 because it simply doesn't belong here. The verse reads, "Mary was the one who had anointed Jesus with perfumed oil and dried his feet with her hair; it was her brother Lazarus who was ill." This event takes place a few days *after* Lazarus is raised. Also, verse 1 tells us that Mary is Lazarus' sister. Obviously an editor redacted and/or rearranged this story without carefully going over the text.

[177] Lazarus is "the one you love", i.e. the beloved disciple who authored the Gospel of John.

*Then, after this, he said to his disciples, "Let us go back to Judea."*
*The disciples said to him, "Rabbi, the Jews*[178] *were just trying to*
*stone you and you want to go back there?" Jesus answered, "Are*
*there not but twelve hours in a day? If one walks during the day,*
*he does not stumble, because he sees the light of this world. But if*
*he walks at night he stumbles because the light is not in him."*[179]
*He said this and then told them, "Our friend Lazarus is asleep*
**but I am going to awaken him" So the disciples said to him,**
*"Master, if he is asleep he will be saved." But Jesus was talking*
*about his death, while his disciples thought he meant ordinary*
*sleep. So then Jesus said to them clearly, "Lazarus has died. And*
**I am glad for you that I was not there, that you may believe. Let**
*us go to him." So Thomas, called Didymus,*[180] *said to his fellow*
*disciples, "Let us also go to die with him."*

*When Jesus arrived, he found that Lazarus had already been*
*in the tomb for four days.*[181] *Now Bethany was near Jerusalem,*

---

[178] As I mentioned above, John uses the somewhat disturbing term, *The Jews*. He even has Jesus calling his own people the Jews, yet he was himself was a Jew. Why would he do that? Most believe it refers either to the Judeans or simply the leaders of the Jews. By the time John wrote his gospel, Christianity was separating from its Jewish roots and becoming a religion unto itself. Also, as I believe, this gospel is a product of the proclamation of the risen Lord Jesus through the communities' prophets. So, it's likely they would refer to the leaders of the Synagogue in their town as the Jews, which would carry over into the Gospel of John. It's sad, because this gospel has certainly been a source of the anti-Semitism which is still prevalent today. .

[179] The ancient people of the Middle East did not understand that light enters through the eyes; rather they believed it was already in the eye.

[180] Didymus in Greek means twin as does Thomas, Ta'oma, in Aramaic.

[181] First century Jews believed that the soul remained with the body for a maximum of four days before departing to the land of the death called Sheol. Sheol was a place of gloom and silence.

*only about two miles away. And many of the Jews had come to Martha and Mary to comfort them about their brother. When Martha heard that Jesus was coming, she went to meet him; but Mary sat at home. Martha said to Jesus, "Lord, if only you had been here my brother would not have died. [But]* **even now I know that whatever you ask of God, God will give to you."**[182] *Jesus said to her, "Your brother will rise."* **Martha said to him, "I know he will rise, in the resurrection on the last day."**[183] ***Jesus told her, "I am the resurrection and the life;*** *whoever believes in me, even if he dies, will live, and everyone who lives and believes in me will never die. Do you believe this?"* **She said to him, "Yes Lord, I have come to believe that you are the Messiah, the Son of God,**[184] *the one who is coming into the World."*

*When she had said this, she went and called her sister Mary secretly saying, "The teacher is here and is asking for you." As soon as she heard this, she rose quickly and went to him. For Jesus had not yet come into the village, but was still where Martha had met him. So, when the Jews, who were with her in the house comforting her, saw Mary get up quickly and*

---

[182]  Notice Martha's faith. Even though her brother is dead she hasn't given up hope.

[183]  Many first century Jews, particularly the Pharisees, believed in an afterlife. At the end of the world God would raise the dead from Sheol and judge them, rewarding the just and punishing the wicked. Jesus gives us a similar view in Matthew 26:31-46.

[184]  Compare this to Matt 16:15. They are almost the exact words of Peter's confession but they are on the lips of a woman! John's Gospel places women in a much more favorable light than Matthew and Mark and even Luke though not as much.

*go out, they followed her, presuming she was going to the tomb to weep there. When Mary came to Jesus and saw him, she fell at his feet and said to him, "Lord, if you had been here, my brother would not have died." When Jesus saw her weeping and the Jews who had come with her weeping, he became perturbed and deeply troubled,[185] and said, "Where have you laid him?" They said to him, "Sir, come and see." And Jesus wept. So the Jews said, "See how he loved him." But some of them said, "Could not the one who opened the eyes of a blind man, have done something so that this man would not have died?"*

*So Jesus, perturbed again, came to the tomb. It was a cave and a stone lay across it.[186] Jesus said, "Take away the stone." Martha, the dead man's sister,[187] said to him, "Lord by now, there will be a stench; he has been dead for four days." Jesus said to her, "Did I not tell you that if you believe you will see the glory of God?" So they took away the stone. And Jesus raised his eyes and said, "Father, I thank you for hearing me. I know that you always hear me; but because of the crowd here I have said this, that they may believe you sent me." And when he had said this he cried out in a loud voice, "Lazarus come out!" The dead man came out, tied hand and foot with*

---

[185] "Perturbed and deeply troubled". The Greek words here are surprising. Its literal translation is, *snorted in spirit;* perhaps meaning that it came from deep within which may indicate Jesus' distaste for death.

[186] Notice the similarity between Lazarus' tomb and Jesus tomb. This is not by accident. Lazarus' resurrection is a prefiguration of Jesus' resurrection.

[187] Repetitive. We have been told twice that Martha is Lazarus' sister. The repetition here indicates, as I said above, a redactor has reworked this narrative.

*burial bands, and his face was wrapped in a cloth. So Jesus*
*said to them, "Untie him and let him go."* [188,189,190]

(Jn 11:1-44)

When I died, and I surely died, I went into the bowels of the earth, Sheol. I was barely aware I still existed. There was only

---

[188]   The Jews did not wrap their dead like a mummy. The burial cloths included tying a piece of cloth around the arms and hands and under the chin. This was to done to prevent the adverse effects of rigor mortis. The body was laid on a shroud which was either on a table or a niche in the tomb. The face cloth would not have been on the body.. It was usually used to transport the body to the tomb and then removed. The bindings are very symbolic. The untying of Lazarus signifies the release from the consequences of sin which is death. For God told Adam in Gen 2:17;"From that tree [of the knowledge of good and evil] you shall not eat; the moment you eat of it you are surely doomed to die."

[189]   The raising of Lazarus is a very complex story, the longest continuous narrative in the gospels except for the Passion. There is no such account in the other gospels leading some scholars to wonder if it is a fabrication. Luke 16:19-31 records the fictitious story of Lazarus and the rich man. However, Lazarus is a beggar and a leper. Still there are some similarities. John mentions Jesus being at the house of Simon the Leper in Bethany although he was rich not poor like Luke's Lazarus. The rich man in Luke's story begs Abraham to have Lazarus go back to his brothers and warn them if they don't change, eternal punishment awaits them. Abraham responds, "If they will not listen to Moses and the prophets, neither will they be persuaded if someone should rise from the dead." (Lk 16:31) The raising of Lazarus made the leaders of the Jews conspire to kill him so it had no positive affect on them.

[190]   According to John 11:47-53, this was the precipitating event that led to the arrest of Jesus and his eventual death. The Synoptic Gospels say it's the cleansing of the temple which led to his arrest, cf Mk 11-18, Matt 21:12-17 and Lk 19:47.

darkness and a terrible silence. There were many others there but I could not tell who they were. Suddenly, I saw a brilliant light. Immediately, my whole body felt warm, almost hot; my pulse pounded against my temples and I knew I was alive again. I lifted the shroud from the top of my body but I had to look away because the light was so bright. Then I realized the stone that sealed my tomb had been rolled away and the light was now shining through the opening. I heard a voice. It was Yeshua commanding me to come out of my tomb. I got up, which was difficult because my hands and feet were tied, so I hobbled to the entrance of the tomb. I saw Yeshua standing there with my sisters and some attendants. He commanded the attendants to untie me and I fell into the arms of my sisters who were sobbing. I turned to Yeshua and said, "Now I believe you raised Yairus' daughter and the widow's son from the dead."

Many of my friends, as well as the disciples, asked me what it was like being dead. I simply told them what I just told you. But then, I said, "The day will come when those who believe in the Son of Man will never go to Sheol for he will raise them up to new life, eternal life where there will be no more suffering, pain or death." I could not believe I said that. It sounded like something Yeshua would say, not me. I felt different. There was no fear, all worry seemed to be gone and I was filled with a joy I had never known. It was like the day I was baptized by Yohanan, only greater.

Six days before Passover, my sisters held a banquet in honor of Yeshua. They were so happy to have me back they were beside themselves and both awed and grateful for what Yeshua had done. His disciples were also invited. We literally killed the fattened calf and the wine flowed and we sang songs and danced. Then Miriam did something that both surprised and disturbed me.

*Mary took a liter of costly perfumed oil made from genuine aromatic nard*[191] *and anointed the feet of Jesus and dried them with her hair; the house was filled with the fragrance of the oil. Then Judas Iscariot, one of his disciples, and the one who would betray him, said, "Why was this oil not sold for three hundred days wages and given to the poor." He said this, not because he cared about the poor but because he was a thief and held the money bag and used to steal the contributions. So Jesus said, "Leave her alone. Let her keep this for the day of my burial. You always have the poor with you but you will not always have me.*[192]

(Jn 12:3-8)

I could not believe what Miriam had just done. She had removed her veil and her head covering in public. A woman could only remove her veil and even her head covering at home among her family but never among strangers. Yeshua was not a stranger but he was not family and his disciples were strangers. I had to look away because the interchange seemed sensual and inappropriate. There was a deep tenderness between them. But, what did Yeshua mean when he said she was preparing him for his burial? He was at the pinnacle of popularity. Surely the leaders of the Jews would not dare arrest him now that he has raised me from the dead. It was certainly proof that Hashem was with him.

---

[191] Nard, also known as spikenard, is a very expensive oil extracted from a plant in India used by the wealthy to anoint the dead. This is a further indication that Lazarus was rich.

[192] Versions of this story are also found in Matthew, Mark and Luke. Matthew and Mark also say the anointing was at Bethany but at the home of Simon the Leper. For Luke, it was at the home of Simon the Pharisee but doesn't name the town. Only John names her as Mary of Bethany eliminating Mary Magdalene who has erroneously been named as the woman. All four sources share common elements indicating they are from the same tradition.

# CHAPTER FIFTEEN

~~~

# The king of glory and his opponents

The next day, Yeshua told Cephas and Andreas to go Bethpage. He said to them:

*"… immediately [upon entering] you will find an ass tethered and a colt with her. Untie them and bring them to me. If anyone should say anything to you, reply, 'The Master has need of them." Then he will send them at once." This happened so that what had been spoken through the prophet might be fulfilled:*

*"Say to daughter Zion*
*Behold your king comes to you*
*meek and riding on an ass,*
*and on a colt, the foal of a beast of*
*burden"*[193]

---

[193] Matthew quotes prophesies from Isaiah 62:11 and Zachariah 9:9. He has misunderstood the prophesy thinking there are two animals when, in the

*The disciples went and did as Jesus had ordered. They brought the ass and the colt and laid their cloaks over them and he sat upon them. The very large crowd spread their cloaks on the road, while others cut branches from trees and strewn them on the road. The crowds preceding him, and those following kept crying out and saying:*

*"Hosanna to the Son of David;*
*blessed is he who comes in the name*
*of the Lord!*
*hosanna in the highest!"*

*And when he entered Jerusalem the whole city was shaken and asked, "Who is this?" And the crowds replied, "This is Jesus the prophet, from Nazareth in Galilee."*

(Matt 21:1-11)

Yudah was elated. "Finally," he said, "he has admitted to all he is the Messiah. The words of prophets have come to pass. Soon, he will usher in his angels. He shall be our King and we shall be free!"

I wasn't so sure. This triumphal entry into Jerusalem was so out of character. Only a few months ago Yeshua was urging everyone not to tell anyone about him. Now he is openly saying he is a King. What will the leaders say? Perhaps he knew this was the time when they were ready to accept him. I had a feeling Yudah was wrong but what happened next made me really wonder about Yeshua's plan, if he indeed had one.

*Jesus entered the temple area and drove out all those engaged in selling and buying there. He overturned the tables of*

---

prophecy, there is only one animal mentioned in two different ways. Mark, who doesn't use this quote mentions only one animal.

*the money changers and the seats of those who were selling doves.*[194] *And he said to them, "It is written:*

*'My house is a house of prayer,'*
*but you are making it a den of thieves."*

(Matt 21:12-13)

The priests, Pharisees and other leaders confronted him:

*"What sign can you show us for doing this?" Jesus answered and said to them, "Destroy this temple and in three days I will raise it up." [They] said, "This temple has been under construction for 46 years,*[195] *and you will raise it up in three days?" But he was speaking of the temple of his body. Therefore, when he was raised from the dead, his disciples remembered that he had said this, and they came to believe the scripture and the word Jesus had spoken.*

(Jn 2:18-22)

Never had I heard Yeshua speak this way. It's as if he was daring them to arrest him. It's, as if, after he raised me from the dead, he gained new confidence. He no longer hid from the authorities and

---

[194] The reason the money changers were there was because only the coinage of Tyre could be used for the purchase of animals used for sacrifice. Part of each transaction went to the Temple priests so they shared in the spoils especially since cheating was common. The moneychangers would fix their scales in their favor. It was a scam which was condoned by the Temple Leaders.

[195] Based on the references in Flavius Josephus (*Jewish Wars* 1,21,1 and *Antiquities* 15,11,1, this took place in 28 A.D. Remember John has the cleansing of the temple early in Jesus' ministry, while in the Synoptic Gospels it's at the end so the dating could be contrived. However, John's placement supports other evidence that Jesus died in 30 A.D.

even challenged them when they confronted him. He had always been self- assured but now he had become almost reckless. Soon, I would discover this was only the beginning of his recklessness.

*The blind and the lame approached him in the Temple area and he cured them. When the chief priests and the scribes saw the wondrous things he was doing, and the children crying out in the temple area, "Hosanna to the Son of David," they were indignant and said to him, "Do you hear what they are saying?" Jesus said to them, "Yes, and have you never heard read the text, 'Out of the mouths of infants and nurslings you have brought forth praise.'?" And leaving them, he went out of the city to Bethany and there spent the night.[196]*

(Matt 21:12-17)

The next morning we went back to the city:

*When he was going back to the city in the morning he was hungry. Seeing a fig tree by the road, he went over to it, but found nothing on it except leaves. And he said to it, "May no fruit ever come from you again. And immediately the fig tree withered."[197]*

(Matt 21:18-20)

---

[196] All the activities in the temple were religious so Jesus' action on the moneychangers was a direct challenge against the authority of leaders of the temple. These leaders were very wealthy and had enormous power. Most scholars believe this was the precipitating event that led to his arrest and execution.

[197] Most likely the fig tree represents the leaders in Jerusalem who have refused to repent and turn to Jesus. As a result they are cursed and will bear no fruit.

Then he told us this parable:

*"There once was a person who had a fig tree planted in his orchard, and when he came in search for fruit on it but found none, he said to the gardener, 'For three years now I have come in search for fruit on it but found none.*[198] *[So] cut it down. Why should it exhaust the soil?' He said to him in reply, 'Sir, leave it for this year also, and I shall cultivate the ground around it and fertilize it; It may bear fruit in the future. If not, you can cut it down.'"*[199]

(Lk 13:6-9)

I was surprised by Yeshua's lack of patience and his anger regarding the fig tree but when he told the parable I realized that it was a symbol of Israel's infidelity to Hashem, particularly the faithlessness of its leaders. I had not realized how disgusted Yeshua was with the temple priests, including the High Priest. But many of us felt the same way. When the brothers Maccabees drove out the Seleucids 150 years ago and established a free Israelite nation, they chose high priests who were not from the line of Zadok, descendants of Moses' brother Aaron. This was contrary to the Law of Moses. If that wasn't bad enough, when the Romans took over, they chose who would be high priest so he was basically a Roman puppet who was handsomely compensated for his loyalty to Rome.

Also, I was now beginning to realize that Yeshua truly believed in the general distribution of wealth so that no one would be

---

[198] The three years may incidentally refer to the length of Jesus' ministry.

[199] Luke softens Jesus' uncharacteristic temper seen above in Matthew by turning the story into a parable. Here, the fig tree could represent Jerusalem or even Israel. John and Jesus have been calling for repentance but to no avail. God is losing patience but the gardener (Jesus?) promises to care for it even more and wins an extension.

without the necessities of life. Such thoughts, coupled with his actions would surely put him in danger of retribution from the leaders in Jerusalem. These men were wealthy and powerful and were not going to relinquish either one. They would certainly do anything to protect them. It was likely only a matter of time before they would act, but Yeshua didn't seem to care.

As soon as we entered the temple area the Scribes and the Pharisees and even the Sadducees immediately confronted him:

*"By whose authority are you doing these things?*[200] *And who gave you this authority?" Jesus said to them in reply, "I shall ask you one question, and if you answer it for me, then I shall tell you by what authority I do these things. Where was John's baptism from? Was it heavenly or of human origin?" They discussed this among themselves and said, "If we say 'of heavenly origin' he will say to us, 'Then why did you not believe him?' But if we say, 'of human origin' we fear the crowd for they all regard John as a prophet." So they said to Jesus in reply, "We do not know." He himself said to them, "Neither shall I tell you by what authority I do these things."*

(Matt 21:23-27)

He then told them this parable.

*"What is your opinion? A man had two sons. He came to the first and said, 'Son, go out and work in the vineyard today.' He said in reply, 'I will not,' but afterward changed his mind and went. The man came to the other son and gave the same order. He said in reply, 'Yes sir,' but did not go. Which of the*

---

[200] This is probably a reference to the triumphal entry into the city, the cleansing of the temple and the healings that ensued.

*two did his father's will?" They answered, "The first." Jesus*
*said to them, "Amen, I say to you, tax collectors and prostitutes*
*are entering the kingdom of God before you. When John came*
*to you in the way of righteousness, you did not believe him; but*
*tax collectors and prostitutes did. Yet even when you saw that,*
*you did not later change your minds and believe in him."* [201]

(Matt 21:28-32)

I could see in the faces of the Scribes and Pharisees that they
were deeply troubled by what Yeshua was saying. Who did Yeshua
think he was judging them? Yet they knew many of the leaders of
our people had rejected the Baptizer. Now they were plotting against
his successor. Soon they would hear a far worse indictment.[202]

*"Hear another parable. There was a land owner who planted*
*the vineyard, put a hedge around it, dug a wine press in it*
*and built a tower. Then he leased it to tenants and went on a*
*journey. The vintage time drew near, and he sent his servants*
*to the tenants to obtain its produce. But the tenants seized the*

---

[201] This parable marks the beginning of three parables that focus on the
judgement of Israel. They have been allegorized by Matthew and probably
have a meaning different from the originals. For example, in its original
form and context this parable simply pointed out the difference between
doing versus saying, which is an important theme in the gospels. Matthew,
however, has added material where the two sons represent the religious
leaders who rejected John the Baptist and the outcasts who accepted him.
In the same way, they accept or reject Jesus.

[202] As we continue to hear these parables we must remember Matthew is
writing his Gospel 60 years after Jesus died. Since then, Jerusalem has
been destroyed; the Pharisees have redefined Judaism and have become the
enemies of the Christians. Consequently, the words of Matthew's Jesus are
likely directed against the Pharisees who are rejecting Matthew's community
and its teaching about Jesus.

*servants and one they beat and the other they killed, and a third they stoned. Again he sent other servants, more numerous than the first ones, but they treated them in the same way. Finally he sent his son to them thinking, 'They will respect my son." But when the tenants saw the son, they said to one another, 'This is the heir. Come, let us kill him and acquire his inheritance.' What will the owner of the vineyard do to those tenants when he comes?" They answered him," He will put those wretched men to a wretched death and lease his vineyard to other tenants who will give him the produce at the proper times." Jesus said to them, "Did you ever read in the scriptures:*

*'The stone which the builders rejected*
*has become the corner stone;*
*By the Lord has this been done,*
*and it is wonderful in his eyes.'*

***Therefore, I say to you, the kingdom of God will be taken away from you and given to a people who will produce its fruit.*** *[The one who falls on this stone will be dashed to pieces; and it will crush anyone on whom it falls.]" When the chief priests and the Pharisees heard his parables they knew he was speaking to them. And although they were attempting to arrest him, they feared the crowds, for they regarded him as a prophet.*[203]

(Matt 21:33-46)

---

[203]  This is another parable that Matthew allegorized. The vineyard is a common image for Israel. The wine press means he's talking about Jerusalem and the servants are the prophets. The son is obviously Jesus. The Old Testament reveals how the prophets were mistreated and notice the son, like Jesus is killed. The parable obliquely predicts the destruction of Jerusalem when the city was destroyed and put in control of the Romans. After a second revolt in 134 A.D. Jews were no longer permitted in the city. Matthew obviously blames the Jews for the destruction of Jerusalem.

Even though the Pharisees were livid, their faces red with rage and their eyes bulging with anger, Yeshua continued:

*"The kingdom of heaven is likened to a king who gave a wedding feast for his son. He dispatched his servants to summon the invited guests to the feast, but they refused to come. A second time he sent other servants, saying, 'Tell those invited: "Behold, I have prepared my banquet, my calves and fattened cattle are killed, and everything is ready; come to the feast." Some ignored the invitation and went away, one to his farm, another to his business. The rest laid hold of his servants, mistreated them, and killed them. The king was enraged and sent his troops, destroyed those murderers, and burned their city.*[204] *Then he said to his servants, 'The feast is ready, but those who were invited were not worthy to come. Go out, therefore, into the main roads and invite to the feast whomever you find. The servants went out into the streets and gathered all they found, bad and good alike, and the hall was filled with guests. But when the king came in to meet the guests he saw a man there not dressed in a wedding garment. He said to him, 'My friend, how is it that you came in here without a wedding garment?' But he was reduced to silence. Then the king said to his attendants, 'Bind his hands and*

---

[204] This parable has been allegorized by Matthew to make it more suitable for his Hellenized Jewish and Gentile audience. The servants represent the prophets of the Old Testament who were basically mistreated and even killed by the Jewish leaders. Like the previous parable, they didn't listen to the prophets and now they are not listening to Jesus. The city is Jerusalem, which was destroyed by the Romans in 70 A.D. The Jews blamed its destruction on the Christians whom they saw as apostates; as I said above, Matthew is blaming them because they did not accept Jesus.

*feet, and cast him outside, where there will be weeping and*
*gnashing of teeth.' Many are invited, but few are chosen."* [205]

(Matt 22:1-14)

The Pharisees and priests left in a huff. "How dare this peasant
speaks to them in this way," they had said. I'm sure they were
plotting against him but they had to figure out a way to turn
the crowd against him. Because Passover was only a few days away
the crowds were much bigger and, I'm sure they realized that if
they simply had him arrested it would cause a riot. That would
involve the Romans and many would die as a result. Soon they
returned, this time with some of the Herodians. [206]

*"Teacher," [they said,] "We know you are a truthful man*
*and that you teach the way of God in accordance with the*
*truth. And you are not concerned with anyone's opinion, for*
*you do not regard a person's status. Tell us then, what is your*

---

[205] This parable is often misunderstood. Like the previous parable it is an
indictment of the Jewish leaders and their lack of faith in Jesus. Again,
in Matthew's opinion, it was because of their rejection of Jesus that God
destroyed the city of Jerusalem. Flavius Josephus said that many believed
Jerusalem was destroyed because the High Priest Ananus instigated the
death of James the Just, brother of Jesus and the head of the Jerusalem
Church who was killed in A.D. 61 or 62.

The wedding garment likely represents the white robe worn by the newly
baptized. Matthew, John and the Didache insist that baptism is required
to become a member of the Church. Like John the Baptist's baptismal
statement, it symbolizes the change of heart and mind that is required to
enter the Kingdom of God.

[206] The Herodians are a mysterious group which has led to much scholarly
debate. Some think they were a separate religious sect who supported the
Pharisees; others think they are simply those who are loyal to Herod.

*opinion: is it lawful to pay the census tax to Caesar or not?"
Knowing their malice, Jesus said, "Why are you testing me
you hypocrites? Show me a coin that pays the census tax."
Then they handed him the Roman coin. He said to them,
"Whose image is this and whose inscription?"*[207] *They replied,
"Caesar's." At that he said to them, "Then repay to Caesar
what belongs to Caesar and to God what belongs to God."
When they heard this they were amazed and leaving him
they went away.*

(Matt 22:15-22)

I realized how clever Yeshua was. Without a doubt they were
trying to entrap him. If he tells them to pay the tax he will offend
the people for we all hate taxation by the Romans. If he tells them
not to pay the tax they will tell the Romans and they will arrest
him. His answer confounds them because it avoids taking sides
and reminds them that everything belongs to God. How this man
amazed me!

Soon after the Pharisees left, some of the Sadducees approached
with another riddle.

*On that day, some Sadducees approached him saying there is
no resurrection.*[208] *They put this question to him saying, Moses
said, "If a man dies without children, his brother shall marry*

---

[207] Images of any kind were forbidden by the Law of Moses, especially human
images. When the Pharisees produce a coin with the image of Caesar on
it, it brings condemnation upon them for the image is graven, meaning
idolatrous, and against the first commandment. As soon as they produce
it, and Jesus asks them about the image, they must have realized they have
been exposed.

[208] While the Pharisees believed in life after death, the Sadducees did not. They
also denied the existence of angels as well as the soul.

*his wife and raise up descendants for his brother.*[209] *Now there were seven brothers among us. The first married and died and having no descendants left his wife to his brother. The same happened to the second and the third, through all seven. Finally the woman died. Now at the resurrection, of the seven, whose wife will she be? For they all had married her." Jesus said to them in reply, "You are all misled because you do not know the scriptures or the power of God. At the resurrection they neither marry nor are given in marriage, but are like the angels in heaven. And concerning the resurrection of the* **dead have you not read what was said to you by God, 'I am the God of Abraham, the God of Isaac and the God of Jacob'.** *He is not the God of the dead but the God of the living."*[210]

(Matt 22:23-32)

Of all those standing there, I was the only one who knew for sure there was life after death. I had experienced the abode of the dead; the Sadducees don't even believe in Sheol, but Yeshua raised me up from Sheol. If Yeshua can raise me to life, after being dead for four days, certainly Hashem can raise us up to eternal life.

In spite of the fact that he had quieted the Sadducees, the Pharisees continued to test him.

---

[209] This is called the levirate marriage law found in Deuteronomy 25:6. The purpose was to continue the family line of a brother who had died and left no descendants.

[210] Jesus, by his response, challenges all the Sadducees' beliefs. They do not know the scriptures because they reject the books of the Prophets and the Writings which imply or, in the case of the Writings, state there is life after death. They don't believe in angels but Jesus says they will be like angels. Finally he quotes Ex 3:6, which is a book they accept, and reminds them that death is not from God, for God only generates life.

*[The Pharisees] gathered together, and one of them [a scholar of the law] tested him by asking, "Teacher, which commandment in the law is the greatest?" He said to him, "You shall love the Lord your God with all your heart, with all your soul and with all your mind. This is the greatest and first commandment. The second is like it: You shall love your neighbor as yourself. The whole law and the prophets depend on these two commandments"*[211]

(Matt 22:35-40).

As we later learned, Yeshua brings an entirely new meaning to the nature of love. Even when he's angry with the leaders of our people there is a kindness that is ever present in him- a look, a smile, eyes that are pleading with them to believe in him, not to prove he's right but so they can know Hashem as he knows him, to really feel his Father's love as he feels it.

After they left Yeshua said:

*"Beware of the scribes, who love to go around in long robes and accept greetings in the market places, seats of honor in the synagogues, and places of honor at banquets. They devour*

---

[211] Both Mark and Luke seem to put these two commandments on equal footing. Matthew clearly does not, indicating that love of God takes primacy. The Gospel of John focuses more on loving one another than he does on loving God. In the ten commandments, three are reserved for God and seven for man. Still, the three are mentioned first. However, Jesus focuses much more on loving one another than he does on loving God. John 15:12 introduces a new commandment, "Love one another as I have loved you." John 15:13 says, No one has greater love than this, to lay down one's life for his friends." St Paul in 1Cor 13 says that love is greater than all things. There is much more on this subject. In fact, the word love is used in the New Testament more than 250 times.

*the houses of widows and, as a pretext, recite lengthy prayers.*
*They will receive a severe condemnation"*

(Mk 12:38-40).

When he said this he was sitting down opposite the treasury observing how the crowd put their money into the treasury.

*Many rich people put in large sums. A poor widow also came*
*and put in two small coins worth a few cents. Calling his*
*disciples to himself, he said to them, "Amen I say to you, this*
*poor widow put in more than all the other contributors to*
*the treasury. For they have all contributed from their surplus*
*wealth, but she, from her poverty, has contributed all she had,*
*her whole livelihood."* [212]

(Mk 13:41-44)

---

[212]  Many of the Christians in the early church were poor. The story contrasts the arrogance and pride of the wealthy scribes mentioned in the previous narrative and supports the first beatitude that the poor are blessed.

~~~

# CHAPTER SIXTEEN

# "Not one stone will be left…"

We decided to return to Bethany and as we were leaving the temple, Ta'oma[213] marveled at its beauty and grandeur.

*Jesus said to him, "Do you see these great buildings? There will not be one stone left upon another that will not be thrown down." Peter, James, John and Andrew asked him privately, "Tell us when will this happen and what sign will there be when all these things are about to come to an end?" Jesus began to say to them, "See that no one deceives you. Many will come in my name saying, 'I am he' and they will deceive many. When you hear of wars and reports of wars do not be alarmed; such things must happen, but it will not be the end. Nation will rise against nation and kingdom against kingdom. There will be earthquakes from place to place and there will be famines. These are the beginnings of the labor pain. Watch out for yourselves. They will hand you over to the courts. You will be beaten in synagogues. You will be arraigned before governors and kings, because of me, as a witness before them. But the gospel must be*

---

[213] The Hebrew name for Thomas

*preached to all nations.*[214] *When they lead you away and hand you over, do not worry beforehand about what you are to say. But say whatever will be given to you at that hour. For it will not be you who are speaking but the Holy Spirit. Brother will hand brother to death, and the father his child; children will rise up against parents and have them put to death. You will be hated by all because of my name. But the one who perseveres in the end will be saved.*[215] *When you see the desolating abomination*

---

[214]    Mark 13 is often called "The Little Apocalypse" because it deals with the destruction of Jerusalem and the end of the world. By the time Mark wrote this, many of the events described have already occurred. The Zealots, basically a group of Jewish terrorists, overthrew Roman rule in the city of Jerusalem and even the surrounding areas in 66 A.D. They turned the city into a fortress believing that God would liberate them from the Romans who were returning with an army to retake the city. In 70 A.D. the Romans under Titus, breached the walls of the city, killed all its inhabitants, took the temple treasures and razed the city. Mark is writing his Gospel during or shortly after this time. It was an horrific time where many of the Jews in the city fought against each other, killed many and even burned their supplies. They not only had to fight the Romans and each other but famine and pestilence as well.

Even before this, Christianity was divided into factions, some which promoted false teaching. Nero persecuted the Christians. The Jews persecuted the Christians as well, hence the fulfillment of Jesus' words about being dragged before kings and judges. Paul mentions being stoned and scourged by the leaders of the synagogue. But this will not be the end of the world because the gospel must be preached to all nations.

[215]    This section most likely refers to the persecution of the Christian community in Rome which is the occasion of this letter. It was the first real persecution of the Church where believers were impaled on tall poles, covered with pitch and set on fire. Others were thrown among the wild beasts in the arena, and still others were crucified. Many renounced their faith, betrayed others and even exposed members of their families to save themselves from death.

*standing where he shouldn't (let the reader understand)* [216] *then those in Judea must flee to the mountains, and a person on a housetop must not go down or enter to get anything out of his house, and a person in the field must not return to get his cloak. Woe to pregnant women and nursing mothers in those days. For these times will have tribulation such has not been since the beginning of God's creation until now nor ever will be.* [217] *If the Lord had not shortened these days, no one would be saved; but for the sake of the elect whom he chose, he did shorten the days. If anyone says to them, 'Look, here is the Messiah! Look, there he is!' do not believe it. False messiahs and false prophets will arise and perform signs and wonders in order to mislead, if that were possible, the elect. Be watchful! I have told you this beforehand."*

(Mk 13:1-23)

Yeshua's words sent shivers through my whole body. Did he really mean what he had said? Could Jerusalem be destroyed again

---

[216] The phrase, "The desolating abomination" comes from the Book of Daniel 9:27, 11:31 and 12:11 where it refers to the desecration of the temple by Antiochus IV who offered pagan sacrifices there in 167-164 B.C. Apparently, Mark's audience understands its present meaning but subsequent generations were not sure. Most likely it refers to the Roman General Titus, who stood in the Holy of Holies, a place reserved strictly for the High Priest. No other Jew could go in there much less a pagan.

[217] There seems to be a shift here that is moving away from the Destruction of Jerusalem (DJ) to the end times; however I believe it is still about DJ. This was probably the most horrific period of Jewish history. Not only was there terrible persecution, but also DJ wiped out the priesthood, the Sadducees and all temple worship and sacrifices. Judaism had to be redefined and it was, in about A. D. 80, by the Pharisees at Jamnia, present day Tel Aviv. It became centered on the law of Moses and its interpretation. The synagogue became the principle place for worship so it is very similar to modern day Judaism. One could say that, for the Jews, DJ marked the end of their world as they knew it.

as it was by the Babylonians centuries ago? Only this time it seemed even worse. The people would not be taken away into slavery. They would all be killed! Fear consumed me as he continued:

> *"But in those days after the tribulation,*
> *The sun will be darkened,*
> *and the moon will not give its light,*
> *and the stars will be falling from the sky,*
> *and the powers in the heavens will be shaken.*
>
> *And then they will see 'the Son of Man coming in the clouds'[218]with great power and glory, and then he will send out the angels and gather his elect from the four winds, from the ends of the earth to the end of the sky. Learn a lesson from the fig tree. When its branch becomes tender and sprouts leaves, you know that summer is near. In the same way, when you see these things happening, know that the end is near, at the gates. Amen I say to you, this generation will not pass away until all these things have taken place. Heaven and earth will pass away, but my words will not pass away."[219]*

(Mk 13:24-31)

Unlike the previous discourse I found this one comforting for it predicted Hashem's victory over evil and if we are among his elect we have nothing to fear because he will gather us up and bring us into his kingdom. I'm still not sure if Yeshua is "the Son of Man" spoken of in Daniel or is he someone else? Yudah, who

---

[218]  A direct quote from Daniel 7:13. It is very similar to Jesus' response to the High Priest when, during his trial, he asked him who he was, cf Mark 15:62.

[219]  Just as anyone can read the processes of nature that summer is near so too believers can read the signs in the world and in the heavens to predict the coming of the Son of Man.

was delighted with his words, again asked him when these things would come to pass. He replied:

> "...of the day and the hour, no one knows, neither the angels in heaven, nor the Son of Man, but only the Father.[220] Be watchful! Be alert! You do not know when the time will come. It is like a man traveling abroad. He leaves home and places his servants in charge, each with his work, and orders the gatekeeper to be on watch. Watch therefore; you do not know when the lord of the house is coming, whether in the evening, midnight, or at cockcrow, or in the morning. May he not come suddenly and find you sleeping. What I say to you I say to all: Watch!"[221]

---

[220] It seems as though Jesus is saying he is not equal to the Father. However, as the second person of the Blessed Trinity he is the same as the Father as taught by the Council of Ephesus in 431 A.D. This is a mystery, since, apparently the human Jesus does not know all things

[221] It should be obvious to the reader that Jesus' prediction of the imminent end of the world did not happen. Yet, practically everyone in the early Church believed that it was going to happen. Both Peter and Paul spoke of it as happening at any moment. If you think about it, why wouldn't they? After all, the crucifixion, resurrection, ascension and Pentecost all took place within 50 days. Jesus would surely return in the next fifty, certainly within a year. That's likely the reason they all left Galilee and settled in Jerusalem where they are told by Jesus to stay, cf Acts 1:4. Perhaps these words of Jesus recorded by Mark are Mark's interpretation of what Jesus really said. The second coming could not be that near because we are told the gospel had to be preached to all nations. When Mark wrote his Gospel the word was perhaps preached in Spain and maybe France but even today it hasn't been preached in the far reaches of the Amazon and some of the other more remote areas of the world. I think the lesson to be learned here is that we can't take apocalyptic (veiled and symbolic) language literally. The main message, whether for Mark's audience or future generations, is we cannot read these passages without knowing the context nor can we use them as a means to predict the future coming of the Messiah, Jesus.

(Mk 13:32-37)

Yeshua's words were very sobering and we walked back to Bethany in silence not sure of what he meant and especially when these things would come to pass. He said they would happen in our generation which means within the next twenty or thirty years. Still, his language was apocalyptic, the language of the seers and prophets. How could he possibly expect us to understand it correctly?

---

One way to explain the discrepancies is that Mark is simply telling us we must not be misled by speculative predictions, yet must always be watchful and alert.

## Chapter Seventeen

~~

# "This is my body…"

The next morning, which was the day before Passover, Yudah left Bethany to go back to Jerusalem. He said he had some personal business to take care of. We later found out that he had gone to see the chief priests to hand Yeshua over to them. We are not sure why he betrayed him but we think he felt that if he forced his hand, Hashem would rescue him and the Kingdom of Hashem would come. Yudah always looked forward to a new Israel which would rule the world. Blinded by ambition, he never understood that Hashem's kingdom was not of this world. The truth be told, at the time, neither did we.

After Yudah had left, Cephas and Yohanan asked Yeshua where we going to eat the Passover. I assumed it would be at my house since we certainly had enough room. However, Jesus said:

*"When you go into the city, a man will meet you carrying a jar of water.*[222] *Follow him into the house that he enters*

---

[222] Usually woman carry water jars so this would be an easily identifiable signal.

121

*and say to the master of the house, 'The teacher says to you, "Where is the guest room where I may eat the Passover with my disciples?"' He will show you a large upper room that is furnished. Make the preparations there.*[223]

(Lk 22:10-13)

He told Martha and Mary to go with them so that they could help prepare the food for the Passover.[224] In the evening we gathered together with Yeshua to partake of the Passover supper.

*When the hour had come he took his place with his disciples. He said to them, "I have eagerly desired to eat this Passover with you before I suffer, for I tell you, I shall*

---

[223] The room must have been very large since Acts 1:13-14 tells us the eleven plus other men, women and the family of Jesus gathered in that room after Jesus ascended.

[224] There is no proof of this but usually woman prepared the Passover meal and participated in it. It was a family celebration so it would have been normal for the female followers of Jesus to help prepare it and also be present for it. However, none of the gospels specifically mention anyone other than the Twelve Apostles. John's Gospel doesn't seem to limit the attendees to the twelve. He refers to those present as disciples, which, throughout his Gospel, often refers to others beside the twelve, however, only members of the twelve are named. So, while the culture of the time period implies others would be present, there is no evidence that this is the case. That said, I have added Eleazar to the group since he is my key witness and the disciple whom Jesus loved.

*not eat it [again] until there is fulfillment in the kingdom of God.*[225]

(Luke 22:14-16)

---

[225] A great deal of explanation is required here. While Matthew, Mark and Luke essentially agree on the details of the Last Supper, John does not. For example, John's account is not a celebration of Passover because it occurs the day before Passover. John 13:1 specifically says this gathering took place before the feast of Passover. John 19:14 says that during Jesus' trial and crucifixion it was the "preparation day for the Passover." Also, there is no institution of the Eucharist in John; instead there is the washing of the feet. John's Jesus gives several long discourses, none of which are found in the Synoptic versions. Scholars through the ages have tried to reconcile these differences, but none satisfactorily. The easiest explanation is that John set the crucifixion on the day before Passover because the lambs for the Passover feast are slaughtered by the temple priests at noon, the same time that Jesus was dying on the cross. This fits with one of John's basic themes that Jesus is "the Lamb of God who takes away the sins of the world". Still, questions remain. Why would John leave out the institution of the Eucharist? It is the singular most important liturgical event in the early Church and one could argue, the New Testament. It is attested by St Paul in 1Cor 11:23-26, which was written at least 15 years before Mark. My response is simple. The author(s) of John's Gospel did not know that tradition. I say this because the early Church was a lot more diverse than once thought. The Gnostics, an early offshoot of the Christianity, make no mention of it in their writings. Most, if not all, were written after John's Gospel. The Didache, a first century Christian document, mentions it but uses completely different words for the blessing of the cup and the bread. In my mind, there is simply no good reason to leave it out unless the tradition was not known.. Some say the foot washing replaces the Eucharist as a symbol for Jesus' suffering and dying. While, I believe that is true, I cannot believe they would leave the Institution of the Eucharist out unless they were not aware of it.

His hour? I remember him talking about my hour. This is obviously a special moment even more special than the Passover itself. And what does he mean by his suffering? What kind of suffering? At the time we had no idea of what was about to transpire during the next several hours.

*[Jesus then] rose from supper and took off his outer garments. He took a towel and tied it around his waist. Then he poured water into a basin and began to wash the disciples' feet and dry them with the towel around his waist.[226] He came to Simon Peter who said to him, "Master, are you going to wash my feet?" Jesus answered and said to him, "What I am doing you do not understand now, but you will understand later." Peter said to him, "You will never wash my feet." Jesus answered and said to him, "Unless I wash you, you will have no inheritance with me." Simon Peter said to him, "Master, not only my feet but my hands and head as well." Jesus said to him, "Whoever has bathed has no need except to have his feet washed, for he is clean all over;[227] so you are clean but not all." For he knew who would betray him; for this reason, he said, "Not all of you are clean." So when he had washed their feet*

---

[226] I decided to add some of John's last supper material to the Synoptic tradition. The washing of the feet is such a moving scene and makes such a powerful statement about what it really means to be a disciple that it can't be ignored. A basic theme in the Synoptic tradition is service, especially to the poor. This is the primary theme of the Gospel of Luke. It is not a central theme in John but this scene really promotes the importance of humility. You cannot be a follower of Jesus without humility. The meek inherit the earth not the proud and arrogant.

[227] Perhaps a reference to baptism but I think it refers to ritual ablutions. Jesus' death on the cross erases sin, so ritual washings are no longer required. It fits with John's replacement theme.

*[and] put his garments back on and reclined at table again, he said to them, "Do you realize what I have done for you? You call me 'teacher' and 'master' and rightly so, for indeed I am. If I therefore, the master and teacher, have washed your feet, you ought to wash one another's feet. I have given you an example to follow, so that as I have done for you, you should also do."*

(Jn 13:1-15)

We all were astounded and deeply moved by what Yeshua had done. But, at first, we were taken aback and even ashamed for him, for we could not believe that our master and teacher would belittle himself so. Slaves washed feet or you washed your own feet but never another's. As he was washing my feet I recalled my sister Miriam anointing his feet and drying them with her hair and I understood why Yeshua did not stop her and actually blessed her because of it. She and perhaps only she, other than Yeshua, understood the meaning of service in the Kingdom of Hashem. After Yeshua had reclined at table we began our celebration in the traditional way by singing a Psalm.[228]

Praise, you servants of the Lord,
praise the name of the Lord.
Blessed be the name of the Lord

---

[228] Psalms 113 to 118 were sung at different times during the Passover supper. Psalm 113, above, obviously is a song of praise. Psalm 114 celebrates Israel's escape from Egypt, 115 recalls their captivity in Babylon, 116 is a song of thanksgiving, 117 a very brief song of praise and 118, another thanksgiving song that celebrates a victory procession of the King of Israel into the temple, reminiscent of Jesus' triumphal entry into Jerusalem a few days before.

both now and forever.
From the rising of the sun to its setting
let the name of the Lord be praised.
High above all the nations is the Lord;
above the heaven's God's glory.
Who is like the Lord our God
enthroned on high,
 looking down on heaven and earth?
He raises the needy from the dust,
lifts the poor from the ash heap.
Seats them with princes,
the princes of the people,
Gives the childless wife a home,
the joyful mother of children.
Hallelujah!

(Psalm 113:1-9)

While we were eating Yeshua became very serious and said:

*"Amen I say to you, one of you will betray me." Deeply distressed at this, they began to say to him one after another "Surely it is not I Lord?" He said in reply, "He who has dipped his hand in the dish with me is the one who will betray me.*[229] *The Son of Man indeed goes, as it is written*

---

[229] A better translation might be, "one who is eating with me" which would be clearer to modern readers. Either way, it's a shocking statement because table fellowship was so important in both Jewish and Christian traditions. Later Judas will greet Jesus in the garden with a kiss another sign of fellowship and brotherhood which was a part of early Christian liturgy. Both emphasize the gravity of the betrayal.

*of him, but woe to that man by whom the Son of Man is betrayed. It would be better for that man if he had never been born." Then Judas, his betrayer, said in reply, "Surely it is not I Rabbi?" He answered, "You have said so."*[230]

(Matt 26: 21-25)

We couldn't believe there was a traitor among us. Why would anyone who was a part of his inner circle betray him? As I mentioned earlier, we found out later, it was Yudah but at the time it was incredulous. Of all of us, Yudah was the most zealous especially with regard to the coming of the Kingdom of Hashem. Such zeal would be his downfall.

*"While [we] were eating, Jesus took bread, said the blessing, broke it, and giving it to his disciples said, "Take and eat; this is my body." Then he took the cup, gave thanks, and gave it to them, saying, "Drink from it, all of you, for this is my blood of the covenant, which will be shed on behalf of many for the*

---

[230] Obviously Judas asked him quietly so the others could not hear him; otherwise they would have certainly responded or tried to prevent him from leaving. This means that Judas must have been sitting next to Jesus. John 13:26-30 has a somewhat lengthy exchange between Judas and Jesus which is also private. In that account, when Judas left the table, the others thought he was told by Jesus to go and give some money to the poor. In John's account the Beloved Disciple is sitting on Jesus' right; Judas must be sitting on his left, which would have been the second most prominent place at the table! The whole betrayal is mysterious because it begs the question, "Why did he betray him?" but all four gospel accounts make it clear that Judas betrayed Jesus.

*forgiveness of sins.*[231] *I tell you from now on, I shall not drink this fruit of the vine until the day when I drink it with you new in the kingdom of my Father."*

(Matt 26: 26-29)

We again did not understand what Yeshua was saying and we were greatly disturbed by it. The bread was *his* body, the wine *his* blood? Drinking any blood was an abomination before the Lord. Surely, he meant this as a symbol. But what did the symbol represent?[232] When was he going to shed his blood? In a battle against the Romans when he ushered in his kingdom? The way he was speaking, the kingdom was coming that night! But how? We certainly weren't an army. The entire evening was shrouded in mystery. Soon we would find out, but it was nothing like we imagined.

---

[231]    Matthew is copying Mark here almost word for word. The earliest attestation of the words of consecration come from St. Paul in 1Cor 11:23-25: *For I received from the Lord what I also handed on to you, that the Lord Jesus on the night he was handed over took bread, and, after he had given thanks, broke it and said, "This is my body that is for you. Do this in remembrance of me." In the same way, also the cup, after supper, saying, "This cup is the new covenant in my blood. Do this, as often as you drink it, in remembrance of me."* Notice, in Paul's account the blessing over the bread and wine are not sequential. The cup is blessed "after supper". The four gospels have placed them together, likely to accentuate the significance that Jesus died for our sins.

[232]    The theology of the transubstantiation, the transformation of the bread and wine into Christ's body and blood, was likely a gradual revelation. The earliest celebration of Mass was called "The breaking of the bread" and was seen as a meal of remembrance, cf Acts 2:42. But, as Christianity gradually moved away from its Jewish roots the idea of Jesus' real presence in the Eucharistic bread and wine slowly emerged. The transubstantiation was discussed by St Augustine and St Ambrose but no formal definition was made until the fourth Lateran Council in A.D. 1215.

As we neared the end of the supper Yeshua concluded with these words:[233]

*"I am the true vine and my Father is the vine grower. He takes away every branch in me that does not bear fruit, and everyone that does he prunes so that it leaves more fruit.[234] You are already pruned because of the word I spoke to you. Remain in me as I remain in you. Just as the branch cannot bear fruit on its own unless it remains on the vine, so neither can you unless you remain in me. I am the vine, you are the branches. Whoever remains in me and I in him will bear much fruit, because without me you can do nothing. Anyone who does not remain in me will be thrown out like a branch and wither; people will gather them and throw them into a fire to be burned. If you remain in me and my words remain in you, ask for whatever you want and it will be done for you.[235] By this is my Father glorified, that you bear much fruit and become my disciples. As the Father loves me so also I love you. Remain in my love. If you keep my commandments,*

---

[233] John has allegorized the following story to make it suitable for his Greek audience. It probably was a simple parable when Jesus originally told it.

[234] Israel is often described as a vineyard that God had provided to be cultivated and cared for. Jesus identifies himself as the vine. Ps 80 identifies the Son of Man as a vine and Sir 24:117 describes Wisdom as a vine.

[235] The basis of the allegory is to demonstrate the importance of the union between Christ and his disciples. They can do nothing apart from him as he is their source of strength and their ability to preach the gospel, which is the way they will bear fruit. If they don't remain united to him the consequences are grave for they, like a poorly connected branch on a vine, will wither and die. Later in John 17:20-23, Jesus prays for unity between himself and the Father and then between himself and his disciples. As he is one with the Father, we are to be one with him.

*you will remain in my love." I have told you this so that my joy may be in you and your joy may be complete. This is my commandment; love one another as I have loved you."*[236]

(Jn 15:1-12)

I had never heard Yeshua speak like this. There was a deep sadness in his eyes and his voice was soft. It was, as though he was going to leave us and he wanted to be sure we remained united to him in a bond of love and fidelity. All the while he had been with us, he'd been instructing us to prepare us for the coming of the Kingdom of Hashem but we never really understood how we were to rule that kingdom. As we were to find out, we were not being prepared to rule but to serve and to bear fruit by proclaiming the good news we had heard from him.

---

[236]  This final commandment seems to supersede all others. It's interesting that throughout his ministry Jesus focuses far more on loving and serving others than he does on loving and serving God. In fact, I believe his fundamental message is that we demonstrate our love for God by loving others, especially if we love as Jesus loves. This means, as we hear throughout all four gospels, true Christians love their enemies, turn the other cheek, do not judge, always forgive and, serve even the poor and the marginalized. It's ironic and sad that so few Christians do these things, especially those in positions of power and authority.

# CHAPTER EIGHTEEN

~

# The Son of Man is betrayed

After singing the final Psalm, Yeshua told us to get up and he led us out to the Mount of Olives.[237] On the way he turned toward us and said:

> *"This night all of you will have your faith in me shaken, for it is written:*
>
> *'I will strike the shepherd*
> *and the sheep of the flock will be*
> *dispersed'* [238]
>
> *but after I have been raised up, I shall go before you in Galilee. Peter said to him in reply, "Though all may have*

---

[237] I chose to leave out most of the discourses found in the Gospel of John which take up four chapters. I did this because they are not found in the other three gospels and as I said above, I believe they are the words of the risen Lord Jesus spoken to the prophets in John's community. My focus in this book is mostly on the gospel proclaimed by the Synoptic Gospels of Matthew, Mark and Luke. The parts of John I did used were those I believed were most likely historical.

[238] The quote is from Zechariah 13:7.

*their faith in you shaken, mine will never be." Jesus said to him, "Amen, I say to you, this very night before the cock crows, you will deny me three times." Peter said to him, "Even though I should have to die with you, I will not deny you." And all the disciples spoke likewise.*

(Matt 26:31-35)

How naïve we were. Especially Cephas. He always had a big mouth, so often speaking without thinking. He was the most foolish of the Twelve and I never admired him until after everything came to pass. He loved to puff out his chest and brag how strong and brave he was, but they were just words. Yet, we were not much different, for we too said foolish things and made promises we didn't keep.

*Then Jesus came with them to a place called Gethsemane,[239] and he said to his disciples, "Sit here while I pray." He took with him Peter, James and John,[240] and began to be troubled and distressed. Then he said to them, "My soul is sorrowful even to death. Remain here and keep watch." He advanced a little and fell to the ground and prayed that if it were possible the hour might pass by him; he said, "Abba, Father, all things are possible to you. Take this cup from me but not what I will but what you will."[241] When he returned he found them asleep. He said to Peter, "Simon, are you asleep? Could you not watch one hour? Watch and pray that you do not*

---

[239] Gethsemane is a Hebrew word which means "oil press" so it was probably the olive grove which was located on the western slope of the Mount of Olives.

[240] Notice how the inner circle of Peter, James and John are privy to this special event, just as they were there for Jairus' daughter and the transfiguration.

[241] Jesus' response is similar to Mary's at the annunciation, cf Lk 1:37.

*undergo the test. The spirit is willing but the flesh is weak."*
*Withdrawing again he prayed, saying the same thing. Then*
*he returned once more and found them asleep, for they could*
*not keep their eyes open and did not know what to answer*
*him. He returned a third time and said to them, "Are you*
*still sleeping and taking your rest? It is enough. The hour has*
*come. Behold the Son of Man is to be handed over to sinners.*
*Get up, let us go. See, my betrayer is at hand."* [242]

(Mk 14:32-42*)*

We awoke with a start. People were screaming and yelling. We
didn't know what was happening until we saw a crowd approaching
with a cohort of priests , Herodians and scribes.

*Judas, one of the Twelve, arrived accompanied by a crowd*
*with swords and clubs who had come from the chief priests,*
*the scribes and elders. His betrayer had arranged a signal with*
*them saying, "The man I shall kiss is the one; arrest him and*
*lead him away securely." He came and immediately went over*
*to him and said, "Rabbi." And he kissed him. At this they laid*
*hands on him and arrested him.*

(Mk 14:43-46)

---

[242] Luke's version is much shorter than Matthew's or Mark's and John does not
recount it at all. Luke's omission is probably because Matthew and Mark
make Jesus too human, probably the same reason John omits it. Luke does
add that the sweat coming from Jesus' head were like drops of blood. It
should be noted that Jesus did not sweat blood. However, these verses are
not in the oldest manuscripts and probably were a later addition. In my
opinion, Jesus is basically having a panic attack. He has, no doubt seen
many crucifixions, and understandably is terrified. It was not only terribly
painful but also humiliating.

I was shocked. There was Yudah, leading the crowd and bringing them to Yeshua. It was bad enough that he betrayed him, but with a kiss? A kiss is a mark of fellowship and love. Was this part of a plan between Yeshua and Yudah? I swear Yudah loved Yeshua as we all did. Why would he turn him over to the Sanhedrin, especially on this, the holiest of nights?

> *One of the bystanders drew his sword, struck the High Priest's servant and cut off his ear.*[243] *Jesus said to them in reply, "Have you come out as against a robber, with swords and clubs to seize me? Day after day, I was with you teaching in the temple area, yet you did not arrest me; but that the scriptures may be fulfilled." And they all left him and fled. Now a young man followed him wearing nothing but a linen cloth about his body. They seized him but he left the cloth behind and ran off naked.*[244]
>
> (Mk 14:47-52)

We were such cowards! Only an hour before we had sworn we would never desert him and then as soon as we were threatened we ran. I stayed a little longer. Since I thought we were going to sleep in the garden I had taken off my tunic and loin cloth so I was dressed in only my linen under garment. When they tried to grab me I ran and they tore the garment from me which allowed me to escape. I returned to the garden, put on my clothes and went back to Jerusalem.

---

[243] John's account says that Peter cut off the ear of the servant and that the servant's name was Malchus, cf Jn 18:10.

[244] The identity of the young man has been the subject of controversy for centuries. The Greek term for youth used here is the same word used to describe the young man at the empty tomb in Mark 16:5. Hence he may be a metaphor for the Christian initiate who. when baptized strips off his old self and then, after baptism, is donned with a white robe to symbolize that he had put on Christ, cf Gal. 3:27 and Eph. 4:24.

# CHAPTER NINETEEN

~~~

# Messiah, son of the Blessed One

I went to the house of Caiaphas, assuming that Yeshua had been taken there. Caiaphas' house was much larger than mine and located in the upper city. It had two courtyards, one at the main level and the other on the lower level where there were three large mikvehs. All the floors were paved with imported stone and tile. There was also a very large room on the main level where the trial was held. This was the room where the Sanhedrin[245] usually met.

When I arrived I saw a large crowd gathered near the house and there, standing in the shadows was Cephas. Since I knew the family and servants of the high priest we were allowed entry into the courtyard and from there we could hear the leaders interrogating Yeshua.[246]

---

[245] The governing body of the Jews. Josephus says the Sanhedrin was first established during the reign of Antiochus the Great, 223-187 B.C. (Josephus, *Ant.* 12.142, 148). It was comprised of seventy one members, Sadducees, Pharisees and scribes. Under the Romans, the Sanhedrin had a great deal of power in Judea but were not authorized to put anyone to death. They could pass a death sentence but technically it couldn't be carried out.

[246] John 18:15 says that the Beloved Disciple was known to the high priest.

*They led Jesus away to the high priest, and all the chief priests and the elders and scribes came together.* [247] *Peter ... was seated with the guards, warming himself at the fire. The chief priests and the entire Sanhedrin kept trying to obtain testimony against Jesus in order to put him to death, but they found none. Many gave false witness against him but their testimony didn't agree. Some took the stand and testified falsely against him, alleging, "We heard him say, 'I will destroy this temple made with hands and within three days I will build another not made with hands.'" Even so their testimony did not agree. The high priest* [248] *rose before the*

---

[247]   The events describing the trial of Jesus have been the subject of considerable debate since the 19th century. Only Matthew and Mark record the trial taking place at night. Luke says it took place during the day. John has separate appearances with Annas at night and Caiaphas in the morning. We have no record of Jewish laws during the first century. The Mishna, a Jewish commentary about rabbinic teaching, written in the late second century, forbids the Sanhedrin to be convened at night or on the eve of the Sabbath nor could the sentence of death be made on the same day as the trial. That would make almost everything about Jesus' trial, as recorded in the gospels, illegal. However, we do not know if the rules described in the Mishnah applied to first century Palestine. Also, Jesus claimed to be a King which was an act of sedition in the eyes of the Romans. The charge of sedition under Roman law was punishable by death. Since Jesus was not a Roman citizen the sentence would have been crucifixion. For millennia the Jews have been held responsible for the death of Jesus which is a terrible error that has resulted in the persecutions and deaths of the Jews to this day. Yes, the leaders of the Jews played a part in it but they were few in number and had no authority to put him to death. People forget: Jesus was a Jew, all his disciples were Jews and until the late 40's A.D. all the followers of Jesus were Jews. Why persecute Jesus' own people? Plainly and simply, the Romans, specifically Pontius Pilate, killed Jesus.

[248]   Most likely, this was Caiaphas who was the son-in-law of Annas who was high priest from A.D. 6 to A.D. 15. but still wielded a lot of power during

*assembly and questioned Jesus, saying, "Have you no answer?*
*What are these men testifying against you?" But he was silent*
*and answered nothing. Again, the high priest asked him and*
*said to him, "Are you the Messiah, the son of the Blessed One?"*
*Then Jesus answered: "I am;*

*and 'you will see the Son of Man*
*seated at the right hand of the Power*
*and coming with the clouds of*
*heaven.'"249*

*At that the high priest tore his garments and said, 250 "What*
*further need have we of witnesses? You have heard the*
*blasphemy.251 What do you think? They all condemned him as*
*deserving to die. Some began to spit on him. They blindfolded*

---

the time of Pontus Pilate. He is also called the high priest in Luke 3:2.

[249] A direct quote from Dan 7:13. Notice too that both the high priest and Jesus refrained from using the divine name substituting it with the "Blessed One" and the "Power".

[250] Tearing one's robe was normally a sign of grief but it was also a sign that one had witnessed blasphemy.

[251] According to Exodus 22:28, blasphemy is reviling God or cursing a ruler of the Jewish people. It could also mean using the divine name. In either case, I see no indication that Jesus has blasphemed. Saying he was the Messiah does not mean he was divine since the Messiah was never believed to be a divine person. As I said above he, like the high priest, refrained from using the divine name. The quote from Daniel indicates he is a divine messenger but so were the prophets. The quote does imply that he was given divine authority to bring judgement upon selected individuals but so are angels as was Moses. That authority does not make him divine. So basically, Mark is saying the trial was a sham. The high priest, along with most of those present, were looking for any excuse to convict him. Lev. 24:10-16 says that blasphemy was punishable by death so it was a way to get rid of Jesus once and for all- so they thought.

*him and struck him and said to him, "Prophesy!" The guards*
*greeted him with blows.*

(Mk 14:53-65)

I was standing just outside the door of the room where Yeshua
was being tried, if you want to call it a trial. I couldn't believe
what they were saying and doing. Yeshua was the most peaceful
and loving man I had ever met. The only times I saw him angry
was when he saw injustice to the poor and the marginalized. He
never lifted his hand against anyone and now they were striking
him, spitting on him. They had completely lost control. And all
the while he just stood there, not fighting back, not cursing them
or spitting back. I remembered his words, "Love your enemies. If
someone strikes on the cheek turn to him the other."

The charge of Blasphemy is death! Hashem certainly would
not let him die. I wondered, *Will the angels come and rescue him?*

Meanwhile Cephas was in the courtyard and I saw one of the
high priest's maids approach him saying:

*You too were with the Nazarene, Jesus." But he denied it*
*saying, "I neither know nor understand what you are talking*
*about." So he went into the outer court. [Then the cock*
*crowed.] The maid saw him and began again to say to the*
*bystanders, "This man is one of them." Once again he denied*
*it. A little later the bystanders said to Peter once more, "Surely*
*you are one of them; for you too are a Galilean."*[252] *He began*
*to curse and swear, "I do not know this man about whom you*
*are talking." And, immediately a cock crowed a second time.*

---

[252] Galileans had a distinct accent of which Judeans often made fun. Matthew's
version of this scene says they recognized Peter because of his accent,
cf Matt 26:73.

*Then Peter remembered the word that Jesus had said to him,
"Before the cock crows twice you will deny me three times."
He broke down and wept.*[253]

(Mk 14:67-72)

I had mixed feelings about Cephas' denial. On one hand, I felt
he deserved to be embarrassed and shown to be a coward because
he was always bragging about himself. On the other hand, I knew
how much he loved Yeshua. He would not forget or get over this
betrayal for a long time but ultimately it would serve to make him
a much stronger disciple.

---

[253] Peter's denial is found in all four gospels. To contrast Jesus' courage before
the high priest and the Sanhedrin, Peter's cowardice is enhanced by his fear
of a maid servant who really has no authority to do anything to him. His
weeping is a traditional sign he has repented and points to God's forgiveness.

# CHAPTER TWENTY

~~~

# Pilate's dilemma

Morning was not far off and the area had become quiet. Many of those in the courtyard were either speaking very softly or had fallen asleep. Yeshua was placed in a dungeon which was basically a pit dug into the bedrock below the house. Prisoners were lowered into the room with a rope so there was no way to escape.[254]

> *As soon as morning came, the chief priests and the elders and the scribes, that is the whole Sanhedrin, held a council.[255] They bound Jesus, led him away, and handed him over to Pilate.[256] Pilate questioned him, "Are you the king of the Jews?" He said in reply, "You say so." The chief priests accused him of many things. Again Pilate questioned him, "Have you*

---

[254] An ancient house in Jerusalem, purported to be that of Joseph Caiaphas has this room.

[255] It seemed like they had already held a council. At alternate translation is "reached a decision" which I think is more plausible.

[256] They led him off to Pilate because, as I mentioned above, they did not have the authority to put anyone to death.

*no answer? See how many things they accuse you of." Jesus gave him no further answer, so that Pilot was amazed.*[257]

(Mk 15:1-5)

Most of the information I received about Yeshua's trial before Pilate was second hand. Pilate was notorious for his cruelty and I feared greatly for Yeshua.

*Pilate then addressed the chief priests and the crowds, "I find this man not guilty." But they were adamant and said, "He's inciting the people with his teaching throughout all Judea from Galilee where he began even to here." On hearing this Pilate asked if the man was a Galilean; and upon learning that he was under Herod's*[258] *jurisdiction, he sent him to Herod who was in Jerusalem at the time. Herod was very glad to see Jesus; he had been waiting to see him for a long time, for he had heard about him and had been hoping to see him perform some sign.*[259] *He questioned him at length, but he*

---

[257] Pontius Pilate was the prefect of Judea from ca. A.D. 25 to 36. As the story unfolds all four Gospels claim that Pilate wanted leniency and didn't want to execute Jesus. This is highly unlikely since Pilate was a tyrant known for his cruelty especially to Jews. Josephus says that when he arrived in Jerusalem he immediately set up Roman standards with Caesar's image on them, a violation against the Jewish law forbidding images. He used temple treasury funds to build an aqueduct and slaughtered many Jews and Samaritans. It was so bad that delegations were sent to Rome who removed him from his post, cf *Ant.* 18.55. Most likely, the evangelists softened the role of Pilate in Jesus' death because their primary audiences were Gentiles and they didn't want to make Rome look bad. It was a way to help keep the peace between the Roman government and the Christians.

[258] Only Luke has Jesus being sent to Herod.

[259] This would be Herod Antipas, the same Herod who beheaded John the Baptist. Jesus obviously disliked him and called him, "that fox", cf Lk 13:32. It's probably why he refused to talk to him.

*gave him no answer. The chief priests and the scribes stood by, accusing him harshly. [Even] Herod and his soldiers treated him contemptuously and mocked him, and after clothing him in resplendent garb, he sent him back to Pilate. Herod and Pilate became friends that day, even though they had been enemies formerly.*[260] *Pilate then summoned the chief priests, the rulers and the people and said to them, "You brought this man to me and accused him of inciting the people to revolt.* **I have conducted my investigation in your presence and have not found this man guilty of the charges you have brought against him, nor did Herod for he sent him back to us. So no capital crime has been committed by him. Therefore I shall have him flogged and then release him."** *But all together they shouted out, "Away with this man! Release Barabbas to us."*[261]

(Lk 23:4-18)

*Now on the occasion of the feast the governor was accustomed to release to the crowd one prisoner whom they wished.*[262] *And at the time they had a notorious prisoner called [Jesus] Barabbas.*[263] *So, when they assemble, Pilate said to them,*

---

[260]   Apparently, their agreement that Jesus did not deserve the death penalty cemented their relationship, cf Lk 23:15.

[261]   Luke takes great pains, by adding a lot of additional material, compared to the other gospel accounts, to make sure the reader understands that Jesus was innocent.

[262]   No evidence of this custom has been found outside the four gospels.

[263]   That Jesus was the first name of Barabbas is found only in a few manuscripts, hence the brackets. The name Jesus, i.e. Yeshua in Aramaic, was a very common name in Palestine; however, the insertion of it in this case may have been for the purpose of irony. Barabbas comes from the Aramaic *bar abba* which means, "son of the father" so it is ironic that the crowd is choosing between Jesus, the true Son of the Father and another son of the father who is a criminal.

*"Which one do you want me to release to you, [Jesus] Barabbas, or Jesus called Messiah?" For he knew that it was out of envy that they had handed him over. While he was still seated on the bench, his wife sent him a message, "Have nothing to do with that righteous man. I suffered much in a dream today because of him."[264] The chief priests and the scribes persuaded the crowds to ask for Barabbas but to destroy Jesus.*

(Matt 27:15-20)

I couldn't believe what I was hearing. How could the crowd cry out for the blood of Yeshua in favor of Barabbas? He was a murderer and an insurrectionist. Surely the chief priests had bribed them for I knew some of them had followed Yeshua. This did not look good for him.

*Then Pilate took Jesus and had him scourged[265]. And the soldiers wove a crown of thorns and placed it on his*

---

[264] Matthew is the only evangelist who refers to Pilate's wife. He also used the dream motif with Joseph when he learns Mary is pregnant and also when they fled to Egypt.

[265] The Jews placed a limit on scourges at twenty plus one but there was no limit for the number of scourges by the Romans. The Shroud of Turin gives us real insight into this. It reveals that Jesus was scourged with a Roman flagrum a short handled whip, which had three leather thongs with dumbbell shaped pieces of metal at each end, which in turn would leave pairs of scourge marks on the victim. Since there are no scourge marks on the arms of the man on the Shroud it is likely he was kneeling with his arms tied to a pole above him. This would allow the soldiers, the Shroud indicates there were two, to have more leverage and inflict more pain. There are well over one hundred pairs of marks indicating Jesus received far more than twenty one scourges.

Note: I have been studying the Shroud of Turin for sixty years and consider myself an expert. I am convinced by the evidence that the Shroud is the burial cloth of Jesus Christ. As a result, during the narrative of the Passion of Christ, many references will be made to the Shroud.

*head*[266] *and clothed him in a purple cloak, and they came up to him and said, "Hail King of the Jews!" And they struck him repeatedly. Once more Pilate went out and said to them, "Look, I am bringing him out to you, so that you may know that I find no guilt in him." So, Jesus came out, wearing the crown of thorns and the purple cloak. And he said to them, "Behold the man!"*[267]

(Jn 19:1-5)

I remember crying out, "Oh my Lord!" I couldn't believe what I was seeing. The loud cry came from the very depths of my gut as I rent my outer garment and fell to the ground in tears. I tried to gaze up at him but I had to turn away. His back was shredded from the lashes, his face bruised and bloody, his nose disjointed. Blood tricked down his forehead from the cap of thorns. He looked so pitiful and alone.[268]

I felt so guilty for abandoning him. We all had promised at the supper we would stand by him. But where were we? I was hiding in the crowd and the others were nowhere to be found. We were cowards, all of us. The woman were off in the distance because they were not allowed to be in the crowd. I'm sure they could see him but not his brokenness.

---

[266] Traditional art portrays this crown as a circlet of thorns typical of the crown worn by a Roman king. The Shroud of Turin depicts it as a cap of thorns which makes more sense since the inscription on the cross clearly states Jesus is the King of the Jews. Jewish kings wore caps. Pollens discovered near the head of the man of the Shroud were found to be from a thorny plant native to the Jerusalem area called *gundelia tournefortii*. It is likely this was used to make the cap of thorns.

[267] The well know phrase "Ecce homo" in Latin, the language Pilate spoke, although he may have said it in Greek, a language the people would have at least somewhat understood. It's likely Pilate did not speak Aramaic.

[268] This description is based again on the Shroud of Turin which graphically displays the extent of the damage done by the beatings and the scourging.

In spite of this, the crowds, egged on by the priests, the elders and the Sadducees cried out, "Crucify him, crucify him!" I was so ashamed of them. They were Israelites like me, my flesh and blood. He had never done anything to harm them. Some of them, I'm sure, he had even healed. And now they were crying out for his blood.

All of us abhorred crucifixion. We had seen so many of our own lining the streets and cursed Rome for their cruelty. Now here they were, demanding that Rome crucify one of their own, not a murderer or thief, but a man of Hashem, a healer and a teacher who loved every single one of them.

Then I thought of his mother. Did she know her son had been arrested and tried by Pilate? Hopefully not. She and her son Yacob and his family had come to Bethany when they heard Yeshua had raised me from the dead. I prayed that she did not come into the city. No mother should ever see her son crucified. Unfortunately, this would not be the case.

> *They all said, "Let him be crucified!" When Pilate saw that he was not succeeding at all, but that a riot was breaking out instead, he took water and washed his hands in the sight of the crowd, saying, "I am innocent of this man's blood. Look to it yourselves." And the whole people said in reply, "Let his blood be on us and upon our children."*[269] *Then he released Barabbas to them... [and] handed him over to be crucified.*
>
> (Matt 27:23-26)

---

[269] This statement is probably most responsible for blaming the death of Jesus on the Jews and the ensuing anti-Semitism down to the present day. It is most unfortunate. Rather than being historical, it was probably devised by Matthew to reflect the conflict between Matthew's community and the Pharisees in the 90's A.D. For a more in-depth understanding of this situation see: Raymond Brown's book, *An Introduction to the New Testament,* (New York, Doubleday, 1997), p. 222.

# CHAPTER TWENTY ONE

~~~

# The way of the cross

It was pitiful as was Yeshua. To see him dragged off to be crucified broke my heart and cut me to my core. They placed the crossbeam on his bloody shoulders and tied his hands to it.[270] Yeshua was a strong man, taller than most of us but, after the severe scourging, he had little strength left. It wasn't long before he fell. He tilted the beam to the side to break his fall and he was able to hit the ground with his knees but then he fell forward on his face. [271]Even the soldiers pitied him.

---

[270] Traditional images showing Jesus carrying the entire cross are ridiculous as it would have weighed several hundred pounds. Also, lumber was scarce in Judea, and since crucifixions were quite common they didn't have any to spare. Normally, the upright section was permanently placed in the ground and the crossbeam was placed into a notch or attached to the top to form a T. Crucifixions varied. Some were crucified facing the cross, others were seated on a horn either with it between their legs or seated on it sideways. Some were nailed and others were tied.

[271] The image on the Turin Shroud depicts bruises on each shoulder indicating that a beam was placed or maybe tied across them. There are also bruises on the knees as well as on the face implying a fall, perhaps more than one. It is also interesting to note that dirt found on the bottom of the foot of the man

*As they led him away they took hold of a certain Simon, a Cyrenian, who was coming in from the country, and after laying the cross on him, they made him carry it behind Jesus.[272,273] A large crowd of people followed Jesus, including many women who mourned and lamented him. Jesus turned to them and said, "Daughters of Jerusalem, do not weep for me; weep instead for yourselves and your children, for indeed the days are coming when people will say, 'Blessed are the barren, the wombs that never bore and the breasts that never nursed.' At that time people will say to the mountains, 'Fall upon us!' and to the hills, 'Cover us!' for if these things are done when the wood is green what will happen when it's dry?" Now, two others, both criminals, were led away with him to be executed.*

(Lk 23:26-32)[274]

I was surprised to see my sister Miriam there and after searching the faces of those around her, I saw my sister Martha with Miriam of Magdala and Yohanna. Then I saw his mother, Miriam with

---

of the shroud contains limestone, which was determined to be identical to that found in Jerusalem.

[272] This certainly indicates how much Jesus was weakened by the scourging. Most men, especially of his height and strength would have been able to carry their cross to its destination.

[273] One of the themes in Luke's Gospel is following in the footsteps of Jesus so the image of Simon following Jesus is that of a disciple following his master. Notice, right after this, many others are following him as well. Cyrene was a city in northern Africa, currently Libya. There was a fairly large Jewish community there.

[274] Both Matthew and Mark say that Jesus was crucified at a place outside the city walls called Golgotha which literally means skull, probably named for the skull-like appearance of the hill. It was a limestone quarry during the time of Solomon; hence the limestone on the foot of the Shroud image.

Miriam the mother of Yacob and Yohanan. *Where were her sons, I wondered? How my heart ached for Yeshua's mother. Her whole body trembled with grief. Her eyes were red from the tears that streamed down her cheeks. She was wailing and lamenting for her son. At least, when they approached the crucifixion site they would make the women stand at a distance so they would not be able to see the brutality of it.*[275]

> *When they reached the place of the skull, they crucified him and the criminals there, one at his right the other on his left.*[276] *[Then Jesus said, "Father forgive them, they know not what they do."] They divided his garments by casting lots.*[277] *The people stood by and watched; the rulers, meanwhile, sneered at him and said, "He saved others, let him save himself if he is the chosen one, the Messiah of God." Even the soldiers jeered at him. As they approached to offer him wine, they called out, "If you are the King of the Jews save yourself."*
>
> (Lk 23:33-37)

---

[275] Crucifixion was a gruesome and humiliating affair. The crucified were naked and often lost control of their bowels. They were in extreme pain and blood was everywhere. It was certainly not a sight for women to see, so they were made to stay about 100 yards away.

[276] The Romans had perfected crucifixion which originated in Persia. They nailed the victim through the wrists and purposely missed any arteries so the victim would not bleed to death. They usually placed a small shelf under the feet so the victim could push himself up to catch his breath. Studies reveal that the crucified died from asphyxiation. That's why breaking their legs hastened death. For a detailed understanding of this see Dr. Pierre Barbet's, *A Doctor at Calvary*, New York, P. J. Kenedy and Sons, 1953.

[277] A typical way for determining ownership or making choices was by lots. Small stones were marked, placed in a container and then spilled on the ground. The first stone to fall marked the winner.

As I stood there and watched them drive the nails through his wrists and then his feet, I wondered how the soldiers could be so cruel. What kind of men would do this? Then, I realized they do it day after day, year after year. They had become immune to its horror. It was all in a day's work. For them, Yeshua was an enemy of Rome and needed to die. They hated us as well, which I'm sure made it easier. Yeshua always said never judge. That's true because it's not because they are Romans that they do this. Everyone is capable of terrible evil. Except Yeshua. I could never imagine him hurting anyone. As I watched him writhing on the cross I wept. I wept not just for him but for everyone with hopes and dreams of being free from hatred and prejudice; from fear and war; from suffering and death.

I wept even more when I heard him asking his Abba to forgive them. How could he be so loving? One of those hanging next to him was blaspheming Hashem and casting insults against the soldiers who crucified them. But then, where was his Abba? Why hadn't he rescued him? Is Hashem going to curse him by hanging him from a tree? How could Israel's Messiah be Adonai's curse?

> *Now, one of the criminals hanging there reviled Jesus saying, "Are you not the Messiah? Save yourself and us." The other, however, rebuking him, said in reply, "Have you no fear of God, for you too are subject to the same condemnation? And, indeed, we have been condemned justly, for the sentence we received corresponds to our crimes, but this man has done nothing criminal. Then, he said, "Jesus remember me when you come into your kingdom." He replied to him, "Amen, I say to you, today you will be with me in Paradise."*
>
> *(Lk23:39-43)*[278]

---

[278] Only Luke has this story. The "good thief" is called Dysmas based on a much later fabricated legend. The story of the good thief is Luke's way of saying that Jesus died for the forgiveness of sins. Notice the good thief never asks

Yeshua was dying! How could he promise the thief paradise? I thought maybe Adonai was going to rescue him, send his angels, usher in his kingdom. I was wrong.

*It was about noon and darkness came over the whole land until three in the afternoon because of an eclipse of the sun.*[279] *Then the veil in the temple was torn down the middle.*[280]

(Lk 23:44-45)

---

for forgiveness for his sins. He simply admits his guilt and recognizes Jesus for who he is and asks him to remember him. For Luke this, apparently, is enough for salvation. It also tells us, in Luke's eyes one does not wait for the final judgement to enter into heaven. This is a much later theology because early on even into the eighties A.D. Christians held the common belief that all would go to the land of the dead and be raised up and judged at the end of the age, cf Matt25:31-46. Most Christians believe in a dual judgement called general and particular. For a better understanding of this see Richard P. McBrien's *The Harper Collins Encyclopedia of Catholicism,* New York, Harper Collins Publishers Inc., 1995, pp 723 -724.

[279] As I mentioned above, John's Gospel places the crucifixion on the day before Passover. At noon the priests slaughtered the lambs for the Passover supper. This is a symbol that confirms John the Baptist's statement that Jesus is the Lamb of God who takes away the sins of the world, for as the lambs are being slaughtered so is Jesus.

[280] This veil separated the main area of the temple from the Holy of Holies, the inner sanctum that only the High Priest was allowed to enter. He always did this on the Day of Atonement to ask God to forgive his own sins and then the sins of the people. The tearing of the veil symbolizes the end of sacrificial worship. Since Jesus died for the sins of all mankind there is no longer any need for sacrifices and sin offerings. As 1 Pet 3:18 says, "Jesus suffered for sins once, the righteous for the sake of the unrighteous, that he might lead us to God," and Heb 9:28 "…so also Christ, offered once to take away the sins of many". The tearing of the veil also symbolized there is no longer a separation between God and mankind. Because of the death of Christ there is a new intimacy between God and his people.

*At three o'clock Jesus cried out in a loud voice, "Eloi, Eloi. lema sabachthani?" which is translated, "My God, my God, why have you forsaken me?"*[281] *Some of the bystanders who heard it said, "Look, he is calling Elijah." One of them ran and soaked a sponge with wine, put it on a reed, and gave it to him to drink saying, "Wait, let's see if Elijah comes to take him down."*

*(Mk 15:34-36)*

I was standing there with Andreas who had finally found enough nerve to come to the site. There was no sign of his brother. I knew Yeshua wasn't calling for Elijah; he was quoting the twenty second psalm. Like the psalmist, who was lamenting his captivity in Babylon, so Yeshua was lamenting his dying on the cross. Again I asked myself, *Where was Hashem?* He truly had abandoned him. Where were the angels who were to come and rescue him? After Yeshua cried out, Andreas and I remembered many of the words of the psalm and spoke them aloud:[282]

"My God I call by day but you do not
answer:
by night but I have no relief.
Yet you are enthroned as the Holy One;
you are the glory of Israel.
In you our ancestors trusted;
they trusted and you rescued them.
To you they cried out and they escaped;

---

[281] Both Luke and John omit this as they find it embarrassing that the Jesus would despair that God didn't seem to care. Mark, always candid, is telling us what happened. He has no agenda; he's not trying to theologize the nature of Jesus.

[282] It was a very common occurrence for the Jews of that time to spontaneously sing or say the psalms.

in you they trusted and were not
disappointed.
But I am a worm, not a man,
scorned by men, despised by the people.
All who see me mock me;
they curl their lips and jeer;
they shake their heads at me:
"You relied on the Lord- let him deliver him;
if he loves you, let him rescue him."
Many bulls surround me;
fierce bulls of Bashan encircle me.
They open their mouths against me,
lions that rend and roar.
Like water, my life drains away;
all my bones go soft.
My heart has become like wax,
it melts away within me.
As dry as a potsherd is my throat;
my tongue sticks to my palate;
you lay me in the dust of death.
Many dogs surround me;
a pack of evildoers closes in on me.
So wasted are my hands and feet
that I can count all my bones.
They stare at me and gloat;
they divided my garments among them;
for my clothing they cast lots."

(Psalm 22:3-9, 13-22)[283]

---

[283] Originally the Psalmist was lamenting his captivity in Babylon in the sixth century B.C. How prophetic, that the words so aptly apply to Jesus' crucifixion.

We were still hoping that Hashem would come and rescue Yeshua but those hopes were quickly dashed.

*Jesus gave a loud cry and breathed his last. When the centurion who stood facing him saw how he breathe his last he said, "Truly this man was the son of God.*[284] *There were also women who were looking on from a distance. Among them were Mary Magdalene, Mary, the mother of the younger James and of Joses and Salome.*[285] *These women had followed him when he was in Galilee and ministered to him. There were also many other women who had come up with him to Jerusalem.*

(Mk 15:37-41)

We walked away sobbing, trying to comfort one another but it was to no avail. I was shaking uncontrollably. How I had loved him! How much he had loved us, all of us, even the traitor Yudah. Yeshua was dead and there was nothing that could bring him back, or so we thought.

---

[284] Mark began his Gospel by saying Jesus was the Son of God; he now has the centurion, a Gentile, affirming it. Many of the believers in the Christian community in Rome were Gentiles.

[285] Mark appropriately has the women standing at a distance. John has Jesus' mother Mary, her sister, Mary Magdalene and Mary of Cleopas standing at the foot of the cross and Jesus giving custody of his mother over to the Beloved Disciple. I doubt this happened for, as I said earlier, women were not allowed within a hundred yards of a crucified victim. Acts 1:14 states Jesus' mother came to the upper room, after Jesus died, with his brothers, i.e. her sons if you accept the scriptural evidence. Personally, I believe Jesus' mother, who is never named in John's Gospel, represents John's community, i.e. the Church, over whom Jesus has given him responsibility. John's Jesus refers to his mother only as "woman". 2 John 1:1 refers to his Church as "the chosen lady" and 1 John often refers to his congregation as "my children". Consequently, the drama at the foot of the cross, in my opinion, is symbolic, and not historical.

# CHAPTER TWENTY TWO

~

# The curse is buried

I told my sisters to take the women to Bethany. They would be safe there. The Romans or the chief priests would never try to harm them anyway. That was not the case for us. But they refused saying they would not leave until Yeshua was properly buried. Crucified victims were normally thrown into a pit where wild animals and birds would tear away their flesh and eat it. My sisters begged me not to let that happen to Yeshua.

I knew a man, Yosef, a Pharisee and a member of the Sanhedrin who was a friend of my father. He greatly admired Yeshua and had tried to intercede on his behalf at his trial. He was a man who had great influence. Yosef negotiated with Pilate to take down the body and, combined with a sizable bribe from me, Pilate gave us permission to take Yeshua for burial. We had to hurry because it was only an hour till sunset and the Sabbath would soon begin.

*Now, since it was preparation day, in order that the bodies might not remain on the cross on the Sabbath, for the Sabbath day of that week was a solemn one, so [they] asked Pilate that their legs be broken and the bodies taken down.*[286] *So the soldiers came and broke the legs of the first and then the other who was crucified with Jesus. But when they came to Jesus and saw that he was already dead, they did not break his legs, but one soldier thrust a lance into his side and immediately blood and water flowed out.*[287] *An eyewitness has testified, and his testimony is true; he knows that he is speaking the truth, so that you also may [come to] believe.*

(Jn 19:31-35)

We were shocked by the soldier's action, one final insult, the coup de gras, so to speak, a violent end to a violent day. Yosef brought a linen shroud with which to wrap the body and carry it to his tomb. Yosef was such a good man. He had offered the use of his own tomb so that the women could properly prepare his

---

[286] As I mentioned above, breaking the legs of the crucified hastened death because they could no longer push themselves up to catch their breath. Once they were unable to do this they died of asphyxiation within a few minutes

[287] The image of the man on the Shroud clearly shows this wound. The size and the elliptical shape of the wound indicate it was made with a *Lancia*, a short Roman spear. The spear entered the body and went through the thoracic wall between the fifth and sixth ribs. Blood likely collected into the plural cavity and, because Jesus was already dead, had separated into its components, thus giving the appearance of both blood and water flowing from his side. 1 Jn 5:6 says that Jesus Christ, "came through water and blood" which probably symbolizes his humanity- either via his birth from the water in the womb or his baptism which marked the beginning of his ministry, and the blood, his redemptive act on the cross. The water and blood could also symbolize the sacraments of Baptism and the Eucharist.

body for burial. We could move the body later to the place where his family was buried.[288]

> *Joseph of Arimathea, a distinguished member of the council, who was himself awaiting the kingdom of God, came and courageously went to Pilate and asked for the body of Jesus.*[289] *Pilate was amazed that he was already dead.*[290] *He summoned a centurion and asked him if Jesus had already died. And when he learned of it from the centurion, he gave the body to Joseph. Having bought a linen cloth, he took him down and laid him in a tomb that had been hewn from rock.*[291]

---

[288]  For those who were wealthy the body was placed in an above ground tomb or a cave. Others were buried in the ground. Once the body had completely decomposed, the bones were placed in a limestone box called an ossuary. If the body was buried, the bones would have to be dug up. Ossuaries usually contained the family name and sometimes an entire family's bones were placed in the same box. A highly decorated ossuary inscribed, *Joseph, son of Caiaphas,* was found In Jerusalem in 1990. Another ossuary inscribed with the words, "James, son of Joseph, brother of Jesus" was discovered in an antiquities store in A.D. 2002. There were no bones in it. Some scholars believe it to be a fake.

[289]  John 19:39 also includes Nicodemus, the member of the council who came to Jesus at night. For a full account of that meeting cf John 3:1-21. Obviously, Joseph could not have taken the body down from the cross and carried it to the tomb by himself. He probably had other help besides Nicodemus. Based on the text at least one other person was the Beloved Disciple.

[290]  It was unusual for the crucified to die in such a short period of time; however John's passion account tells us how badly Jesus was beaten so surely he was weakened by the substantial loss of blood. Also, he simply may have lost his will to live and stopped pushing up with his legs and, as a result, suffocated.

[291]  Joseph of Arimathea and the wound in the side are the main components of the legend of the Holy Grail, purportedly the cup Jesus used at the last

*Then he rolled a stone against the entrance of the tomb. Mary Magdalene and Mary the mother of James watched where he was laid.*

(Mk 15:43-47)

Yosef brought a cart with him. We covered Yeshua's face with a cloth, as was our custom,[292] and placed the body in the cart. We wheeled Yeshua to the tomb which was only a few hundred yards away. Then we carried his body into the tomb and placed it on a table upon which there was a long linen cloth. We removed the

---

supper. The legend comes from the late twelfth century and is associated with the Knights Templar. It was modified somewhat during the next three centuries. It basically states that Joseph of Arimathea went to the cross with the cup Jesus used at the Last Supper and collected the blood of Jesus as it flowed from his side. The legend says the holder of the cup receives great spiritual blessings, including eternal youth. It is, of course a romantic legend but most legends are based on a factual incident. I believe the Holy Grail is the Shroud of Turin. The Shroud was used by Joseph to wrap the body of Jesus and certainly collected a great deal of his blood, most of which, as the Shroud depicts, came from the wound in Jesus' side. It was stolen by the Knights Templar from a church in Constantinople in about 1204 A.D. and venerated by them. The details of this assumption are complicated and not appropriate for this treatise. I use it solely as a point of interest.

[292] The face cloth is called a sudarium and was used out of respect for the dead. There is a sudarium, purported to be the cloth that covered the face of Jesus, in the Cathedral of San Salvador, in Oviedo, Spain. While there is no image on it, the blood stains match the stains on the face of the man of the Shroud of Turin. It's provenance goes back to Jerusalem in A.D. 570 where it is said to have been kept in a cave. Pollens found on the cloth are indigenous to Jerusalem and North Africa where the clothe was take prior to the invasion of Palestine by the Persians in A.D. 614.

face cloth and covered his body with the rest of the shroud.[293] We then rolled a large stone across the opening of the tomb.

Since it was the Sabbath, my sisters and the other women could not travel back to Bethany so we decided to go to the upper room where we had celebrated the Passover. When we arrived, we found the eleven were also there. Except for Andreas and Cephas, they had been hiding there the whole time. We greeted each other with relief that we were all safe but with a deep sadness and a great deal of confusion . I could sense embarrassment and guilt in those who ran away and hid. None of us could believe Yeshua had died.

The unspoken question remained within all of us. "If he truly was the Messiah how could he have been hung from a tree?" We all knew the words of scripture, "Cursed is the one who is hung from a tree."[294] How could Hashem's curse be the Messiah? And yet, if Yeshua was cursed how could he be so filled with love? How could he heal and drive out demons? How could he have raised me from the dead?

Matthew said what most of us were thinking. "He made fools of all of us," he said. "We were duped! The Pharisees were right. They saw him for what he really was- a magician and a false Messiah, like so many before him." All but the women nodded in agreement.

Miriam of Magdala, speaking for all of them, said, "I don't care what your scripture says. He was my master. He loved me like no other has ever loved me. Not with carnal desire but with deep affection; the same way he loved all of you."

---

[293] The Shroud of Turin is believed to be this cloth. It is a piece of expensive linen, 14 feet three inches long and 42 inches wide. It contains the frontal and dorsal image of a crucified man with markings identical to those described in the passion narrative. The evidence for its authenticity is more than compelling. I believe it is the actual burial cloth of Jesus Christ. For a more in depth understanding of the Shroud, go to Shroud.com, a website which contains extensive material about the Shroud.

[294] Cf Dt 21:23

Then she looked at each of us, her dark eyes flashing and we could see the fury in them. "You are all cowards. Where were you when he was condemned? Were you there when they dragged him through the streets? Were you there when they nailed him to that cross? Only Eleazar saw it all but even he ran away when Yeshua was arrested. Andreas came but only at the end when he thought he might be safe. You disgust me. All of you. Instead of feeling sorry for him you're feeling sorry for yourselves and you have the audacity to blame him!" She spat at us with such contempt we all looked away in shame.

Cephas had been sitting in the corner of the room by himself quiet and very still but Magdalene's words cut him to his core and he began to shake uncontrollably. Tears blurred his eyes as he cried out, "I denied him! Three times I denied him, just as he predicted. I betrayed him. I'm no better than Yudah!"

*Yudah*! I had forgotten about him for the moment. Where was he and why had he betrayed Yeshua? I asked the others about him and Magdalene said that he had hanged himself.[295] *Poor Yudah*, I thought. He was so zealous for the kingdom but it was his zeal that destroyed him. So many times Yeshua told us that the kingdom was already here, in our midst and that it was not of this world but Yudah never heard those words. But we were no different. Yacob and Yohanan wanted to sit at his right and left. What had he said to them? "Can you drink the cup that I drink?" Was this the cup he was talking about? The cup of martyrdom? But then, I thought, what did his death have to do with the kingdom? He was dead. Like they had said, it was over. But soon, we would find out it was not over. It was only just beginning.

---

[295] Only Matthew and Luke speak of Judas' demise. Matt 27:5 says he hanged himself, Acts 1:18 says he was killed in a fall, which was either an accident or a suicide. The text is not clear.

# CHAPTER TWENTY THREE

～

# "He has been raised, he is not here."

The next morning, even before we awoke, some of the women decided to go to the tomb to properly wash and anoint Yeshua's body. There was no time to do it yesterday because it was Shabbat. Cleopas and Miriam, Yeshua's uncle and aunt were preparing to leave. They were going back to their home in Emmaus. Right before they left, the women came back with an incredible and shocking story.

*When the Sabbath was over, Mar y Magdalene, Mary, the mother of James and Salome brought spices so that they might anoint him. Very early, when the sun had risen on that first day of the week, they came to the tomb. They were saying to one another, "Who will roll back the stone for us from the entrance to the tomb?" When they looked up they saw that the stone had already been rolled back; it was very large. On entering the tomb they saw a young man, clothed in a white robe, and they were utterly amazed. He said to them, "Do not be amazed. You seek Jesus of Nazareth, the crucified. He has been raised, he is not here. Behold the place where they laid him. But go and tell his disciples and Peter, 'He is going*

*before you to Galilee; there you will see him, as he told you.'"*
*Then they went out and fled the tomb, seized with trembling*
*and bewilderment. They said nothing to anyone, for they were*
*afraid.*

(Mk 16:1-8)[296]

---

[296] The resurrection accounts differ a great deal. For Mark, there are no appearances and the women tell no one. Matthew's account is very similar to Mark's but, rather than a man dressed in a white robe an angel appears to the women. Then, Jesus appears to them and commissions them to tell the disciples he will go before them in Galilee where he appears on a mountain telling them to preach the Gospel and baptize in the name of the Trinity. Luke tells us about the two on the road to Emmaus, how the woman found the empty tomb, that Jesus appeared to Peter and finally he appears to the whole group, showing them his wounds. He then leads them to Bethany where he ascends into heaven. All of this happened on Easter Sunday yet, Luke, who also wrote Acts, tells us Jesus appeared to his disciples for forty days before he ascends into heaven. Finally, John's Jesus appeared first to Mary Magdalene at the tomb then to the disciples on Easter Sunday and again a week later for the benefit of Thomas. Finally, in John 21 an additional appearance in Galilee was written down by another author, where we hear the well-known "Peter do you, love me?" dialogue. In 1 Cor 15:5-7, St. Paul tells us Jesus appeared to Cephas, then the twelve, then to more than five hundred, his brother, James and then all the apostles. Why are there so many differences and apparent contradictions? We need to remember, except for 1 Corinthians, the Gospels were written forty to seventy years after the events and none of the authors were eyewitnesses. Paul was not an eyewitness in the sense of Jesus' bodily resurrection but, no doubt, he received his information firsthand and wrote his testimony only about twenty five years after Jesus rose. However, we must remember through the course of up to seven decades, stories will change, some of them on purpose, to fit the writer's agenda. Yet, if they weren't diverse, I would be more suspicious about their authenticity than if they agreed in every detail which to me would imply collusion.

We stood there in disbelief. Cleopas called their story nonsense, "A bunch of foolish women," he said,[297] and he and Miriam left to go back to their home in Emmaus.

After we hastily said our goodbyes I said to the others, "Perhaps, someone has stolen the body or perhaps Joseph of Arimathea moved it to a more permanent tomb." He certainly had no idea where we were since he had never seen the upper room. So, there was no way for him to tell us. The others agreed that it was the most likely explanation. Still Cephas and I decided to go and inspect the tomb. Miriam of Magdala insisted on going with us for she was certain the body had been stolen.

*Peter and the other disciple[298] went out and came to the tomb. They both ran, but the other disciple ran faster than Peter and arrived at the tomb first; he bent down and saw the grave cloths there, but did not go in. When Peter arrived after him, he went into the tomb and saw the burial clothes there, and the cloths that covered his head, not with the burial cloths but rolled up in a separate place.[299] Then the other disciple went in, the one who had arrived at the tomb first, and he saw and*

---

[297]  One of the proofs for the authenticity of the resurrection narratives is that women are portrayed as the first witnesses. A woman's testimony at that time was considered frivolous and certainly not acceptable in a court of law. It is argued, rightly so, that if the evangelists had contrived these stories they certainly would have not made women the first eyewitnesses.

[298]  Most scholars believe the other disciple was the Beloved Disciple, i.e. Eleazar in my case.

[299]  The shroud of Turin indicates that aside from the shroud itself there were other cloths; a cloth placed over the top of the head and tied under the chin to keep the mouth closed; another tied around the wrists to keep the arms together during rigor and perhaps a third tied around the ankles. As I stated above, another cloth called the sudarium or face cloth would have

*believed. For they did not yet understand the scripture that he
had to rise from the dead. Then the disciples returned home.*

(Jn20:3-10)

The body was not stolen. A thief would not have carefully
folded the grave cloths and set them aside. Even his shroud was
folded back on itself. Joseph of Arimathea must have moved
the body. *But why would he not leave it in the shroud?* Perhaps
he washed the body and anointed it yesterday evening. But then
why all this secrecy? The women had told him they were going to
wash and anoint the body this morning. It was indeed a mystery.

*Now that very day, two of them were going to a village seven
miles from Jerusalem called Emmaus, and they were conversing
about all the things that occurred. And it happened that while
they were conversing and debating, Jesus himself drew near
and walked with them, but their eyes were prevented from
recognizing him.[300] He asked them, "What are you discussing
as you walk along?" They stopped, looking downcast. One of
them, named Cleopas,[301,302] said to him in reply, "Are you the*

---

been placed over the face when the body was removed from the cross, a sign
of reverence, and then taken off when the body was placed in the tomb.

[300] It seems that the risen Jesus looked different for there are other occasions
when he wasn't recognized at first, cf Jn 20:15 and 21:4. I believe the risen
Lord could only be recognized by people of faith as is the case today. The two
on the road to Emmaus had lost their faith in Jesus and until he opened their
eyes (remember faith is a gift from God) they did not know who he was.

[301] Legend says that Cleopas was the brother of Joseph and therefore Jesus' uncle.

[302] As I alluded to above, I believe Cleopas was traveling with his wife Miriam.
Jn 19:25 mentions Mary, the wife of Cleopas standing at the foot of the
cross. Assuming we are talking about the same Cleopas, then it is logical
that he would be traveling back home with his wife.

*only visitor to Jerusalem who does not know of the things that have taken place therein these days?" And he replied to them, "What sort of things?" They said to him, "The things that happened to Jesus the Nazarene, who was a prophet mighty in deed and word before God and all the people, how our chief priests and rulers handed him over to a sentence of death and crucified him. But, we were hoping that he would be the one to redeem Israel; and besides this, it is now the third day since this took place. Some women from our group, however, have astounded us: they were at the tomb early this morning and did not find his body; they came back and reported they had had indeed seen a vision of angels who announced that he was alive.[303] Then some of those with us went to the tomb and found things just as the women had described but him they did not see.[304] And he said to them, "Oh how foolish you are! How slow of heart to believe all the prophets spoke! Was it not necessary that the Messiah should suffer these things and enter his glory? Then beginning with Moses and all the prophets, he interpreted to them what referred to him in all the scriptures.[305] As they approached the village to which they were going, he gave the impression that he was going on farther. But they urged him, "Stay with us for it is nearly*

---

[303] Luke's version of the empty tomb is similar to Matthew's account but with more detail. It is very different from John's account which includes two angels and Jesus' apparition to Mary Magdalene.

[304] Cleopas' testimony is what scholars call a creedal statement as it contains some of the fundamental beliefs of the early Church. Notice the similarities to the Apostles Creed.

[305] The early Church used this method to prove to potential converts, and against detractors, that Jesus was the Messiah. Of the four evangelists, Matthew, ascribes to this method the most, using over 130 quotations from the Hebrew Scriptures.

*evening and the day is almost over."*[306] *So he went in to stay
with them. And it happened that, while he was with them at
table, he took bread and said the blessing, broke it and gave it
to them. With that their eyes were opened and they recognized
him, but he vanished from their sight. Then they said to one
another, "Were not our hearts burning [within us] while he
spoke to us on the way and opened the scripture to us?"*[307]
*So they set out at once and returned to Jerusalem where they
found gathered together the eleven and those with them who
were saying, "The Lord has risen and has appeared to Simon.
Then the two recounted what had taken place on the way
and how he was made known to them in the breaking of the
bread.*[308,309]

(Lk 24:13-25)

---

[306] Hospitality was a very important in the early Church and was part of the
Jewish tradition as well.

[307] The important lesson here is, before we read the scripture, we need pray to
the Holy Spirit to allow Jesus, who is the Word of God, to speak to us and
with a good commentary, teach us the meaning of the scripture passages we
are reading.

[308] The phrase, "The breaking of the bread" is the term use for the celebration
of the Eucharist in the early Church, cf Acts 2:46.

[309] This is one of my favorite stories in the Gospels but I question its accuracy.
I call it a parable in action because it has the qualities of a parable. It is
also an allegory, so it is similar to the allegorized parables we find in the
Gospels, especially in Luke, but one which has been put into an historical
context. The footnote in "The Catholic Study Bible" regarding this passage
says, that "the episode is primarily catechetical and liturgical rather than
apologetic." This means it's instructional rather than arguing a religious
doctrine. I believe the story has an historical basis which Luke stylized to
instruct his community and demonstrate the importance of liturgy, most
especially the Eucharistic meal.

By the time Cleopas and Miriam had returned to tell us their story Yeshua had appeared to Peter.[310] Yet, most of us were still having a very difficult time believing it. Jesus certainly appeared to be dead; he wasn't drugged as some would later say and I saw the lance pierce his side. When we took him down from the cross and took him to the tomb there was no sign of life. In fact, we had to tie his hands because rigor was starting.[311]

I was raised from the dead but I wasn't scourged and pierced so badly that I had lost almost all of my blood. I also was not hung from a tree. I was not accursed of God. That's what troubled all of us the most. Still Peter swore he saw him as did Cleopas and Miriam.

Then there was Miriam from Magdala. She had gone back to the tomb swearing to find out who had stolen his body. She had yet to return and we began to worry about her. It was late in the evening when she walked into the upper room. Her face was radiant and she couldn't stop talking.

> [312]*Mary stayed outside the tomb weeping. And as she wept, she bent over into the tomb and saw two angels in white sitting there, one at the head and one at the feet where the body of Jesus had been. And they said to her, "Woman, why*

---

[310]  There is no occasion in any of the gospels where Jesus appears only to Peter, except incidentally in the Emmaus story. St Paul in 1 Corinthians 15 says Jesus appeared to Peter first but there is no description of the appearance. Personally, I find that strange. Except for James, the one Paul calls the brother of Jesus, Peter is the most important person in the early Church; although some would argue it was Paul. However, Paul never saw Jesus in the flesh nor the risen Lord in the flesh. He only saw him in visions similar to what he experienced on the road to Damascus. I find it strange there is no isolated appearance of Jesus to Peter.

[311]  The Shroud of Turin indicates that the body was in the state of rigor mortis.

[312]  Only John has this story.

*are you weeping?" She said to them, "They have taken my Lord, and I don't know where they laid him." When she said this, she turned around and saw Jesus there, but did not know it was Jesus. Jesus said to her, "Woman, why are you weeping? Whom are you looking for?" She thought he was a gardener[313] and said to him, "Sir, if you carried him away, tell me where you have laid him and I will take him." Jesus said to her, "Mary!"[314] She turned and said to him in Hebrew, "Rabouni," which means Teacher. Jesus said to her, "Stop holding on to me, for I have not yet ascended to my Father. But go to my brothers and tell them, 'I am going to my Father and your Father, to my God and your God.'"[315]*

(Jn 20:1-17)

Miriam said that after she saw Yeshua she was so elated she just walked all over Jerusalem laughing and singing. She wanted to dance and celebrate but she finally came to her senses and remembered Yeshua's commission to tell us he has been raised from the dead. "He promised he would see us soon," she said.

"Are you sure Miriam," I asked.

---

[313] In John's version of the burial, the tomb for Jesus was in a garden. Mankind fell from grace in a garden; now he is restored to grace in a garden. The similarity is not accidental.

[314] John 10:1-30 says Jesus knows his sheep and they know him. They recognize his voice. Only when Jesus says, "Mary" does she recognize him.

[315] It sounds as though Jesus will be ascending into heaven very soon yet, John has several appearances of Jesus over the next few weeks. In Luke's Gospel, Jesus rises, appears to his disciples and ascends into heaven on Easter Sunday yet, as I said above, Acts, also written by Luke, has Jesus appearing for forty more days. As I said earlier, the resurrection narratives are conflicting, confusing and sometimes contradictory. Part of this, I think, is due to their inability to describe supernatural events which are often outside the realm of normal experience.

"As sure as I see you standing before me," she said. "And he wasn't a vision because I fell down at his feet and hung on to them. He was real, as real as he had been before he died. Yet, he was different. At first, I didn't recognize him and I don't know why. It was as though I was only seeing a shadow, an outline and then, as soon as he said my name, everything became clear and there he was, standing before me smiling like he always smiled."

Four people had now seen him, all on different occasions but for some reason I still doubted. Of all of us I should have doubted the least. If Yeshua had raised me from the dead why can I not believe that Adonai had raised him from the dead? Perhaps, most of all, why hadn't he appeared to me? I, along with Andreas, knew him before any of them. As I was pondering these things there he was standing before us!

> ...he stood in their midst and said to them, "Peace be with you." But they were startled and terrified and thought they were seeing a ghost. Then he said to them, "Why are you troubled? And why do questions arise in your hearts? Look at my hands and feet, that it is myself."
>
> (Lk 20:36-39)

How did he get into the room? The doors were locked. He looked right at me when he spoke but he wasn't perturbed. He was smiling because he saw how frightened we were. Only Peter, Miriam of Magdala, Cleopas and Miriam were not afraid, obviously because they had already seen him. Still, I was stunned. It looked like him, it sounded like him, so it must be him! My heart was pounding, my mind was confused but a great joy welled up within me. It was really him! He continued to speak.

> Jesus said to them again, "Peace be with you. As the Father has sent me, so I send you. And when he had said this he

*breathed on them and said them, "Receive the Holy Spirit.*
*Whose sins you forgive are forgiven them, and whose sins you*
*retain are retained.*[316]

(Jn 20:21-23)

Ta'oma[317] was not with us when Yeshua appeared and said he
would not believe it was Yeshua until he examined his wounds.
Ta'oma doubted many things Yeshua told us and often he would
leave the group for long periods of time to reflect on what he had
said. He also looked like Yeshua and because Ta'oma wasn't with
us, some believed that he was trying to trick us- that it was Ta'oma
not Yeshua who appeared to us.[318]

*Thomas, called Didymus,*[319] *was not with them when Jesus*
*came. So the other disciples said to him, "We have seen the*
*Lord." But he said to them, "Unless I see the mark of the nails*
*in his hands*[320] *and put my finger into the nail marks*[321] *and*

---

[316] Jesus gives them the Holy Spirit here as this is John's version of Pentecost.
The breathing of Jesus on them recalls the Garden of Eden when God
breathed life into Adam. Luke 24:36-49 also has a similar account of Jesus
appearing to the disciples in the upper room but his version of Pentecost is
very different as found in Acts 2:1-4.

[317] Aramaic for Thomas.

[318] Ta'oma means twin in Aramaic and there is a legend that claims Thomas and
Jesus were twins which makes little sense in view of the virginal conception
and other evidence.

[319] Didymus means twin in Greek.

[320] The Shroud of Turin clearly indicates Jesus was nailed through the wrists
not the hands as translated here, however, *keipa*, the word for hand in
Greek, is not specific and can include the wrist as well as the forearm. An
ossuary, containing the bones of a crucified victim in Jerusalem named
Yohanan, has a nail between the radius and the ulna.

[321] This is the only place in the gospels that indicates Jesus was nailed to the cross.

*put my hand in his side, I will not believe."*[322] *Now a week later, his disciples were again inside and Thomas was with them. Jesus came, although the doors were locked, and stood in their midst and said, "Peace be with you." Then he said to Thomas, "Put your finger here and see my hands, and bring your hand and put it into my side, and do not be unbelieving but believe." Thomas answered and said to him, "My Lord and my God!" Have you come to*[323] *believe because you have seen me? Blessed are those who have not seen and have believed."*

(Jn 20:24-29)

---

[322] One of the important themes, not only in John's Gospel, but also his letters, is that Jesus rose from the dead in the flesh. This was done to refute the Gnostic heresy called Docetism or perhaps in this case pre-Docetism. The Docetics were a second century philosophical group of Gentile Christians who believed that Jesus only appeared to have a physical body. He was pure spirit. This stemmed from the belief that all material things were evil. As a result, Jesus could not have a body since the divine could not exist in something evil. So Jesus could not have suffered and died on the cross and the risen Jesus could not been corporal. It is likely that Docetism emerged from John's community. Docetism was part of a larger group who were called Gnostics, the name derived from the Greek word *gnosis* meaning "knowledge". The Christian Gnostics believed that salvation came through knowledge not faith as St Paul claimed. They also believed there were two or more gods and the Father of Jesus, who was good, was different from the Hebrew god who was evil. The Hebrew god created matter which was evil since all material things are corruptible; Jesus' Father created the spirit which was eternal and good. There were many different Gnostic cults, Hebrew, Christian and pagan. Christian Gnostics were a powerful force to be dealt with by the Church in the second and third centuries.

[323] This story is for all those who were not present to see the risen Lord which is basically all of John's community. They believe not because they have seen him but through the eyes of faith which, of course includes all of us.

It is true! Hashem has raised Yeshua from the dead and he lives again! All the sadness we felt when he was crucified was gone. But he kept leaving us. When would he return again and for what purpose? Would he be ushering in his kingdom and, if so, what role would we play? I was not one of the twelve so what did he have in mind for me? There was still so much that we did not know or understand?

## CHAPTER TWENTY FOUR

≈

# "He is going before you to Galilee"

The women said he told them he would go before us in Galilee, so Cephas decided we should go back to Lake Galilee and wait for more instruction. Many of us felt we could not remain in Jerusalem for we had outlived our stay in the upper room. However, Ezra, the owner of this most luxurious and very large house said we could stay as long as we wished, so some of our group stayed behind. We still feared the authorities and worried that if they found us we too might be arrested and punished. So, Cephas, Andreas, the sons of Zebedee, Ta'oma, some other disciples and I set off to Cephas' house in Bethsaida. Several hours after we arrived, Cephas couldn't sleep and decided to go fishing so we went with him.

*After this, Jesus revealed himself again to his disciples at the sea of Tiberias.*[324],[325] *Together were Simon Peter, Thomas*

---

[324] The Roman name for Lake Galilee.

[325] John 21 was added by someone other than the original evangelist. The author even tells us in Jn 21:24 that he is not the Beloved Disciple. He probably added it because there were no appearances of Jesus in Galilee in

*called Didymus, Nathanael from Cana in Galilee, Zebedee's sons and two others of his disciples. Simon Peter said to them, "I am going fishing." They said to him, "We will also come with you." So they went out and got into the boat, but that night they caught nothing.*[326] *When it was already dawn, Jesus was standing on the shore, but the disciples didn't realize it was Jesus.*[327] *Jesus said to them, "Children have you caught anything to eat?"*[328] *They answered him, "No." So he said to them, "Cast the net over the right side of the boat and you will find something." So they cast it and were not able to pull it in because of the number of fish. So, the disciple whom Jesus loved said to Peter, "It is the Lord!" When Simon Peter heard that it was the Lord, he tucked in his garment, for he was lightly clad and jumped into the sea. The other disciples came in the boat, for they were not far from the shore, only about a hundred yards, dragging the net with the fish. When they climbed out on shore, they saw a charcoal fire with fish on it and bread. Jesus said to them, "Bring some of the fish you just caught." So Simon Peter dragged the net ashore full of one hundred and fifty three large fish.*[329] *Even though there*

---

John's Gospel. Jesus had promised to go before them in Galilee but, as we shall see, this was not the only reason it was added.

[326] It was common for commercial fishermen to fish during the night on Lake Galilee.

[327] Later in the narrative we are told Jesus was about 100 yards from the shore so, unlike the two on the road to Emmaus, he didn't prevent them from recognizing him; he was simply too far away.

[328] Nowhere in any of the gospels can I recall Jesus calling the disciples "children", however, the writer of John's epistles refers to his congregation as "My children". You also find the use of this term in the Didache.

[329] Notice the exact number is given so it was probably symbolic. St Jerome claimed that Greek Zoologists catalogued 153 species of fish. Jesus called

*were so many the net was not torn. Jesus said to them, "Come have breakfast." And none of the disciples dared to ask him, "Who are you?" because they realized it was the Lord. Jesus took the bread and gave it to them, and in like manner the fish.[330] This was now the third time Jesus was revealed to his disciples after being raised from the dead.[331]*

(Jn 21:1-14)

Yeshua told us to go back to Jerusalem and he would meet us at the Mount of Olives[332] where he would give us our final instructions. But before he vanished from our sight he took Cephas aside and he said to him:

*"Simon son of John, do you love me more than these?" He said to him, "Yes Lord, you know that I love you." He said to him, "Feed my lambs." He then said to him a second time, "Simon, son of John, do you love me?" He said to him, "Yes Lord, you know that I love you." He said to him, "Tend my sheep." He said to him a third time, "Simon, son of John do you love me?" Peter was distressed that he asked him a third time, "Simon, son of John, do you love me?" and he said to him, "Lord, you know everything: you know that I love you."*

---

the Apostles to be fishers of men and to preach the gospel to the ends of the earth so the fish could represent all people.

[330] Notice the similarity to the Eucharistic meal which is not reported by John.

[331] The third time according to John's Gospel.

[332] The Mount of Olives overlooks Jerusalem across the Kidron river valley. Many important events in Jesus' life took place there. According to Matthew his triumphal entry into Jerusalem started from there, cf Matt 21; 1-11; he wept for Jerusalem there and his agony in the Garden of Gethsemane was at the foot of the mount, cf Matt 26:30; and, of course he will ascend into heaven from there, cf Acts 1:12.

*[Jesus] said to him, "Feed my sheep." Amen, amen I say to you, when you were younger, you used to dress yourself and go where you wanted; but when you grow old, you will stretch out your hands, and someone else will dress you and lead you where you do not want to go."*[333] *He said this signifying by what kind of death he would glorify God. And when he had said this, he said to him, "Follow me."*

*Peter turned and saw the disciple following whom Jesus loved, the one who had reclined upon his chest during the supper and said, "Master, who is the one who will betray you?" When Peter saw him, he said to Jesus, "Lord, what about him?" Jesus said to him, "What if I want him to remain until I come? What concern is it of yours? You follow me." So the word spread among the brothers that that disciple would not die.*[334]

---

[333] The threefold confession of Peter contrasts his threefold denial. There are two different Greek words for love used here by John's Jesus, *agape* and *philia*. The former means divine love and the second means brotherly love. The first two times Jesus uses *agape* so he's basically asking Peter, "Do you love me as God loves me?" Both times Peter uses *philia*, meaning, "I love (*philia*) you as a brother." Finally, Jesus simply asks him if he loves him as a brother and Peter responds in kind. Then Jesus tells Peter he is going to be a martyr. By the time this Gospel was written every believer knew Peter died a martyr's death. Legend says he was crucified upside down. Jesus is telling Peter he will eventually love him with divine love since, as Jesus says in Jn 15:13, "No one has greater love than this, to lay down one's life for one's friends." Peter will indeed love Jesus as he has loved him.

[334] Apparently, there was a common belief that the beloved disciple would not die until Jesus returned but by the time the Gospel was written he had died. This is one of my arguments that Lazarus, i.e. Eleazar, is the Beloved Disciple. Why would they think that he wouldn't die? Unless he had already died! They concluded that Jesus would not have raised him from the dead only to let him die again, especially in light of his second coming.

*But Jesus had not told him he would not die, just "What if I want him to remain until I come?"*

(Jn 21:15-23)

Yeshua left Cephas and walked over to me and to my surprise embraced me and told me how much he loved me. I was surprised and deeply moved by his display of affection and I told him so. "I always thought I was never good enough for you Lord," I said.

Yeshua looked at me inquisitively saying, "Eleazar, why would you think that?"

"Well," I said, "you asked me to sell everything and follow you. I followed you but I kept all my possessions save that which I used to fund your mission. Also, you didn't make me one of the twelve. I was never privy to any of the special events that you shared with Cephas, Yacob and Yohanan."

"And you were jealous, my friend?" he asked.

"Yes Lord, I suppose I was."

"Eleazar," he said, "Truly, truly I say to you, I have always loved you more than the others. And you know why?" I shook my head. "Because you and only you were always faithful to me. I never had to worry that you might leave me. And you surely showed it the night and day of my passion.

When I was arrested only you remained behind until they tried to seize you. But you came back to Caiaphas' house and witnessed my trial. You were there in the morning when I was arraigned by Pilate and you stood in the crowd which was crazed by the poison the leaders fed them. You walked with me as I carried my cross and you stood there unafraid and watched me die. Then, with Joseph, you took me down from the cross, and took me to my tomb. Only you, only you, Eleazar were there for me. Only you stayed until the end. You are indeed my beloved disciple.

A lump welled up in my throat and tears flowed freely down my face. My eyes were almost blinded by those tears and when they cleared Yeshua was gone.[335]

We journeyed back to Jerusalem and as the Lord commanded we went out to the Mount of Olives. Many of his followers joined us because they had heard he was raised from the dead so the number was well over one hundred.[336]

*When they had gathered together they asked him, "Lord, are you at this time going to restore the kingdom of Israel?"[337] He answered them, "It is not for you to know the time or the seasons that the Father has established by his own authority. But you will receive power when the Holy Spirit comes upon you, and you will be my witnesses in Jerusalem, throughout Judea and Samaria, and to the ends of the earth." When he had said this, as they were looking on, he was lifted up and a cloud took him from their sight. While they were looking intently at the sky, as he was going, suddenly two men dressed in white garments stood beside them.[338] They said, "Men of Galilee, why are you standing there looking at the sky? This Jesus who has been taken up from you into*

---

[335] This scene is the only scene in this book, thus far, that is pure invention. There is no evidence anywhere that such a conversation took place however what is said is true. The Beloved disciple was with Jesus from the beginning to the end of his passion. He was also with him during his entire ministry.

[336] 1 Cor 15:6 says the Jesus appeared to 500 brothers (probably meaning men and women) however, numbers are usually greatly exaggerated in both the Old and New Testaments.

[337] Notice that they still believe him to be a political leader who will bring Israel to its former glory. After all that has happened they still didn't get it.

[338] When Mary Magdalene entered the tomb she encountered two angels dressed in white garments, cf Jn 21:1.

*heaven will return in the same way as you have seen him going into heaven.*[339] *Then they returned to Jerusalem from the mount called Olivet, which is near Jerusalem, a Sabbath day's journey away.*[340]

(Acts 1:6-12)

---

[339] This is likely the reason the disciples set up their base community in Jerusalem with the belief that Jesus was going to return by descending onto Mount Bethany.

[340] The distance one is allowed to travel on the Sabbath, about two thirds of a mile.

# CHAPTER TWENTY FIVE

~~

# A Spirit of wind and fire

We left Olivet with mixed emotions. We were sad to see him leave but there was the anticipation that he would return soon. So we went back to the upper room as instructed and prayed for the coming of the Holy Spirit. Miriam, his mother and his brothers joined our group in the upper room.[341] There were about 70 of us there so it was quite crowded.[342]

Cephas stood up and said:

*"My brothers, the scripture had to be fulfilled which the Holy Spirit spoke beforehand through the mouth of David, concerning Judas, who was a guide for those who arrested Jesus. He was numbered among us and was allotted a share*

---

[341] cf Acts 1:14. Four brothers are mentioned by name in Mk 6:3, James, Joses, Judas and Simon. After Herod Agrippa killed James the brother of John in A.D. 44, James, called the Just, whom Paul called the Lord's brother, became the head of the Jerusalem Church and remained so until his martyrdom in A.D. 62.

[342] Acts 1:15 says there was 120 people there which is probably an exaggeration since, as I stated above, numbers were usually inflated. It was likely symbolic, meaning 10 people per apostle who could proclaim the Gospel to the world. It's doubtful the upper room was big enough even to hold seventy people much less 120.

*in this ministry. He bought a [parcel of land, which was the wages of his iniquity, and falling headlong, he burst open in the middle and all his insides spilled out. This became known to everyone who lived in Jerusalem, so that the parcel of land was called in their language*[343] *'Akeldama', that is Field of Blood.*[344] *For it is written in the Book of Psalms*

*'Let his encampment become desolate, and may no one dwell in it.'*
*And:*
*'May another take his office.'*

*Therefore, it is necessary that one of the men who accompanied us the whole time the Lord Jesus came and went among us,*[345] *beginning from the baptism of John until the day he was taken up from us, become with us a witness to his resurrection." So they proposed two, Joseph called Barsabbas and Matthias.*[346] *Then they prayed, "You Lord, who know the hearts of all, show which one of these two you have chosen to take the place in this apostolic ministry from which Judas turned away to go to his own place." Then they gave the lots to them, and the lot fell on Matthias, and he was counted with the eleven apostles.*

(Acts 1:15-26)

---

[343]  The term, "their language" is strange since the word *Akeldama* is Aramaic, the same language the apostles spoke. It is a clue that the evangelist was not a Jew.

[344]  Matt 27:3-10 claims the field was a potter's field purchased by the temple priests with the 'blood money" which Judas returned.

[345]  Peter is implying that the Twelve knew Jesus since John's baptism. This, to me, is an indication that the Twelve knew Jesus before they were officially called in the gospel narratives.

[346]  The replacing of Judas had symbolic value since the Twelve were seen as replacing the twelve tribes of Israel in the new Kingdom of Israel instituted by Jesus. In Luke's case this would be the Church. Matthias is never mentioned anywhere else in the New Testament.

There I was, left out again. I fulfilled all the requirements; in fact I was the first to follow Yeshua. But I must admit I took it well. Yeshua had promised he had a charge for me and whatever it might be I was ready to accept it. I just didn't understand how I was going to know what it was or when it would happen.

The next day, we celebrated the Feast of Pentecost,[347] the day that Yeshua promised to send us his Holy Spirit. So we set aside extra time for prayer to prepare. That morning we awoke with a great sense of anticipation. We were not disappointed.

*When the time for Pentecost was fulfilled, they were all in one place together. And suddenly, there came from the sky a noise like a strong driving wind, and it filled the entire house in which they were. Then there appeared to them tongues as of fire, which parted and came to rest on each of them. And they were all filled with the Holy Spirit and began to speak in different tongues, as the Spirit enabled them to proclaim.*[348,349]

---

[347] Pentecost, originally known as *The Feast of Weeks*, was a harvest feast that occurred fifty days after Passover. According to Lev 23:15-17, loaves of bread were baked with wheat from the spring harvest. These were offered up to the Lord as the first fruits of said harvest. It, of course, became a Christian feast because of the descent of the Holy Spirit.

[348] No doubt, Luke has stylized his account to accentuate the importance of this event. I have no doubt that this event took place but Luke has dramatized it with symbols. The wind represents the powers from heaven, e.g. "a mighty wind blew across the waters" at the creation. Fire represents the power of God on earth. God appeared to Moses in a burning bush, cf Ex 3:2. John the Baptist says that Jesus will baptize with the Holy Spirit and fire, cf Lk 3:16. Speaking in tongues is a gift of the Holy Spirit, cf 1 Cor 12, usually babbling, but often real languages of which the speaker is unfamiliar.

[349] It is important to note that without the actions of the Holy Spirit the followers of Jesus would likely have failed in their mission to evangelize

*Now there were devote Jews from every nation under heaven staying in Jerusalem.*[350] *At this sound they gathered in a large crowd, but they were confused because each one heard them speaking in his own language. They were astounded and in amazement they asked, "Are not all these people speaking Galileans? Then how does each of us hear them in his own native language? We are Parthians, Medes and Elamites, inhabitants of Mesopotamia, Judea and Cappadocia, Pontus and Asia. Phrygia and Pamphylia, Egypt and the districts of Libya near Cyrene as well as travelers from Rome, both Jews and converts to Judaism, Cretans and Arabs, yet we hear them speaking in their own tongues about the mighty acts of God.*[351] *They were astonished and bewildered, and said to one another, "What does this mean?" But others said scoffing, "They have had too much wine."*[352]

*(Acts 2:1-13)*

---

the Roman Empire. The presence of the Spirit with its signs and wonders provided confirmation that what they said about Jesus and his ministry was true. Something extraordinary had happened in the past because extraordinary things were happening in the present. A good example is found in Acts 8:9-25. It's about a magician named Simon whose magic was so impressive his followers thought he was divine. But when he saw the power of the Holy Spirit, he was so amazed by its powerful manifestations he offered a large sum of money to purchase that power.

[350] Obviously an exaggeration. It could not have been from *every* nation.

[351] For Luke the regions named are symbolic as they probably represent all the nations or areas where people had converted to Christianity up to the time of Luke.

[352] The Holy Spirit is sometimes symbolized by wine because of this verse. When Jesus converted water into wine, cf John 2:1-11, the water symbolized the Old Covenant with its required ritual ablutions and the wine the New Covenant, the age of the Holy Spirit.

The experience of the Holy Spirit was indescribable. The wind was so loud, far louder than in the storm we experienced at sea. Then there was the fire. It was blazing over our heads but there was no heat. Instead, it fell like rain drops and rested over our heads. It almost felt like it was washing us clean of sin- like a baptism but without the immersion. We were all filled with such joy, like nothing I have ever experienced and we were immersed in the love of Hashem. We danced and sang the last three Psalms[353] praising Hashem with all our hearts. We were so filled with love we hugged each other, even the women,[354] telling everyone how much we loved them. I thought about Yudah, and even though I never liked him, I felt love for him now and prayed for his soul.

We went out onto the porch, as many as could fit, singing and dancing and soon a large crowd came to investigate the commotion. Then Cephas, who somehow had become our spokesman, quieted the crowd and us. He addressed them with these words.

*"You who are Jews. Indeed all of you staying in Jerusalem. Let this be known to you, and listen to my words. These people are not drunk, for it is only nine o'clock in the morning. No, this is what was spoken through the prophet Joel:*

*'It will come to pass in the last days,'*
*God says,*
*'that I will pour out a portion of my spirit*
*upon all flesh.*
*Your sons and daughters shall prophesy,*
*your young men shall see visions,*
*your old men will dream dreams.*

---

[353] Psalms 148 to 150 are the final songs which praise God for all things.
[354] Hugging a woman who was not a family member was unacceptable in that culture.

*Indeed, upon my servants and my handmaids*
*I will pour out a portion of my spirit in those*
*days, and they shall prophesy.*
*And I will work wonders in the heavens*
*above and signs on the earth below:*
*blood, fire, and a cloud of smoke.*
*The sun shall be turned to darkness*
*And the moon to blood,*
*before the coming of the great and*
*splendid day of the Lord.*
*And it shall be that everyone shall be*
*saved who calls on the name of*
*the Lord.'*[355]

*You, who are Israelites, hear these words. Jesus the Nazarene*
*was a man commended to you by God with mighty deeds,*
*wonders and signs, which God worked through him in your*
*midst, as you yourselves know. This man, delivered up by the*
*set plan and foreknowledge of God, you killed using lawless*
*men to crucify him. But God raised him up, releasing him*
*from the throes of death, because it was impossible for him to*
*be held by it.*[356] *For David says of him:*

---

[355]   The quote is taken from Joel 3:1-5 and sets the model by which the earliest
disciples would preach the gospel. They will search the Old Testament and find
quotations which apply to Jesus and use them to show Jesus is the Messiah
who was raised from the dead and will return to judge the world. This quote
reveals that the age of the Holy Spirit has come, a sign of the end times.

[356]   Peter's sermon is basically a summary of the gospel that will be preached by
him and others. It is called the *kerygma* in Greek, which means "teaching".
It includes the basic message about Christ crucified, how his suffering and
death was part of God's plan, that they witnessed the risen Christ and he
is glorified and sits at God's right hand. The listeners respond by repenting

*'I saw the Lord before me;*
*with him at my right hand I shall not*
*be disturbed.*
*Therefore my heart has been glad and*
*my tongue has exulted;*
*my flesh, too, will dwell in hope,*
*because you will not abandon my soul*
*to the nether world,*
*nor will you suffer your holy one to*
*see corruption.*
*You have made known to me the paths of life;*
*you will fill me with joy in your presence.'*[357]

*My brothers, one can confidently say to you about the patriarch David that he died and was buried, and his tomb is in our midst today. But since he was a prophet and knew that God had sworn an oath to him that he would set one of his descendants upon his throne, he foresaw and spoke of the resurrection of the Messiah, that neither was he abandoned to the nether world, nor did his flesh see corruption. God raised this Jesus; of this we are all eyewitnesses. Exalted at the right hand of God, he received the promise of the Holy Spirit from the Father, and poured it forth, as you both see and hear. For David did not go up into heaven, for he himself said:*

*'The Lord said to my Lord,*
*"Sit at my right hand*
*until I make your enemies your*
*footstool."'*

---

and being baptized. Their reward is the reception of the Holy Spirit, its gifts and salvation. It's the earliest form of the Apostles Creed.

[357] The quote is from Psalm 16:8-11 which, at the time, was believed to have been written by King David.

*Therefore, let the whole house of Israel know for certain that God has made him both Lord and Messiah, this Jesus whom you crucified."*

(Acts 2:14-38)

I stood there stunned. Where did Cephas get all this? He was an illiterate fisherman and hardly a man of eloquence. Most of the time, he swore and cursed. His accent was even crude for a Galilean. Yet, here he was, quoting scripture and speaking to these people with persuasiveness and authority. It was as if Yeshua was speaking through him.[358]

When the crowd heard him they were deeply touched and asked Cephas and the rest of us:

*"What are we to do my brothers?" Peter [said] to them. "Repent[359] and be baptized, every one of you, in the name of Jesus Christ[360] for the forgiveness of your sins; and you will receive the gift of the Holy Spirit. For the promise is made to you and to your children and to all those far off, whomever the Lord our God will call. He testified with many other*

---

[358]  In his last supper discourses, cf John 14-17, Jesus tells his disciples that the Advocate, i.e. the Holy Spirit, will teach them everything they need to know and speak through them on their behalf. Peter's eloquence and knowledge of the scriptures is the result of his being possessed by the Holy Spirit. As I mentioned earlier, I believe without the gifts of the Holy Spirit the Church would not have survived.

[359]  The word used here for "repent" is a form of the Greek word, *metanoia*, which was the same word used by John the Baptist and Jesus. It literally means to turn one's life around and fix one's eyes on God.

[360]  Notice Peter asks them to be baptized in the name of Jesus. Baptism in the name of the Trinity came much later.

*arguments and was exhorting them, "Save yourselves from*
*this corrupt generation." Those who accepted this message*
*were baptized; and about three thousand persons were added*
*that day.*[361]

(Acts 2:37-41)

Cephas' proclamation moved me greatly and I developed
a new respect for him. He was always bold and outspoken but
his words were never carefully chosen. As I said earlier, he was
a braggart and a buffoon. But today, like Yeshua, he spoke with
authority and for the first time I sensed an air of humility. No
doubt his denial had greatly humbled him. But during these past
few days, he had become a natural leader, one who I now looked
up to. No doubt the coming of the Holy Spirit had changed him
and, not only him, but also all of us as well. Like Cleopas and
Miriam, when they encountered the risen Lord on the road, our
hearts burned within us, burned with the fire of love, burned with
the desire to proclaim the gospel.

---

[361] The number of converts is likely a large exaggeration. Baptism was by
immersion and they were not near a river or lake. Most residences in
Jerusalem had Mikvahs but it's very unlikely they would open them up
for public use. They could not possibly have baptized that many people.
Most people don't realize how small the Church was in the first century.
For example, it is estimated that there were only 50 to 100 people in the
community in Corinth when Paul wrote his letter to them in the early
50's and it was probably his largest church. Acts ends with Paul's Roman
imprisonment in A.D. 62. I believe the total number of Christians at that
time was about 3000 and this scene in Acts is referring to that number,
which, in Luke's eyes was large. Josephus (Ant.17.42) says there were only
6000 Pharisees in the entire Empire in A.D. 30 and they had been around
for almost 200 years.

~~~

# CHAPTER TWENTY SIX

# Eleazar, apostle to Rome

Late in the afternoon, on that same day, I went out to the Mount of Olives to pray and ponder all that had taken place since Yeshua was raised from the dead. It was a very hot day but as I was praying a cool breeze came up from the west and as I enjoyed the relief from the heat. Suddenly I was surrounded by an intensely bright light and I heard Yeshua calling my name,, "Eleazar, Eleazar," he said.

"Yes Lord," I answered.

"Take my Gospel to Rome," he replied.[362]

---

[362] No one knows who brought the gospel to Rome. It certainly was not one of the Twelve because, if there was any evidence at all, the Church would have certainly used it to support it's teaching about the papacy and apostolic succession. Jews in Rome were converted early. Claudius expelled the Jews from Rome in A.D 49. Suetonius, a Roman historian said that the reason for the expulsion was, "at the instigation of Chrestus", likely a misspelling of *Christus*, meaning there must have been some very heated controversy among the Jews in Rome over the messiahship of Jesus. Priscilla and Aquila were part of that expulsion and Acts 18:2-3 mentions they joined Paul in Corinth. Most likely the community in Rome was founded well before that

I questioned him but he simply repeated the same words, "Take my Gospel to Rome."

Finally, I asked, "Who am I that I should be able to do this?"

He simply replied, "I will be with you." Then he left me alone as the sun was setting into the Great Sea.

I got up and hurried to get back to Jerusalem before it was dark. When I arrived I told no one of my vision. The next morning I gathered my sisters and journeyed back to Bethany. On the way, I recounted my experience on the Mount of Olives and I told them that Yeshua had commissioned me to go and preach the Gospel to the Jews in Rome. To my surprise they were delighted and insisted on going with me. Then I told them what Yeshua had said to me long ago about selling all my possessions. I asked them how they felt about that and they again surprised me be saying that I could not continue to deny that calling.

Miriam looked at me with great intensity and said, "My brother, what did Yeshua tell us? 'Don't worry about what you are to eat or wear. Your life is more important than food and your body more than clothing. If Hashem can clothe the grass in the fields and cares for the sparrows that fly in the air how much more will He care for you?' People who have little faith go after such things Eleazar. Possessions don't last. God will provide."

---

but there is no evidence at all as to who founded it. I took the liberty of making it Lazarus and his sisters. It seems strange that, outside the gospels, they are never mentioned. Going to Rome early in the history of the Church could certainly account for that. There is a legend that says Lazarus went to Cyprus where he encountered Paul and Barnabus and then later became a Bishop in Cyprus. While there is no sound basis for this legend, it implies that Lazarus did not stay in Palestine.

Martha said, "The Twelve gave up everything for him and they have managed. You can give part of the money you receive from the estate to the Brethren.[363] They certainly will need it."

I realized my sisters had far more faith than I. They are indeed a blessing for me plus their witness gave me the confidence I needed to do our Master's will.[364]

. . .

Several months have passed since my sisters and I made the decision to proclaim the gospel in Rome. We used this time to complete the sale of our estate and make preparations for our trip. I sent a letter to my Uncle Samuel and Aunt Sarah who lived in the capital of the Empire. I received his response yesterday and he has graciously offered us lodging for as long as we wished. We haven't seen them since my father died and are looking forward to renewing our relationship. Samuel is my father's younger brother. I am uncertain as to how he will accept the gospel. Many Jews, especially our leaders in Jerusalem refuse to accept that a crucified man could be the Messiah.

We have decided to delay our trip till the spring since winter is approaching and traveling by sea to Cyprus and then on the Rome would be dangerous. In the meantime, we will continue to live with the Brethren in Jerusalem. We all celebrate the Sabbath in the temple and on Sunday, which we now call the Lord's Day in honor of Yeshua, we break bread in remembrance of him and we tell our stories about him and his gospel.

---

[363] The early Church in Jerusalem called themselves the Brethren who followed the Way. The Greek word for brethren is gender inclusive.

[364] As I mentioned earlier there was a common belief that when two or three people of faith agree on something it is the will of God.

These are the stories I have shared with you and will share with those in Rome. If Yeshua doesn't return soon, I will write down some of these stories as a proclamation of his gospel so they will never be forgotten. In the meantime, I ask you to pray for me and my sisters. We are about to enter a new chapter in our lives and we know not what lies ahead. I am comforted by Yeshua's last words to me, "I will be with you," and even though I cannot see him I can feel his presence and I am certain he will never abandon me.

In the meantime, we all pray that he returns soon to establish his kingdom, a time when he will rule as Messiah and Lord, a time of everlasting peace and joy because,

The spirit of the Lord shall rest upon him
a spirit of wisdom and of understanding.
A spirit of council and of strength,
a spirit of knowledge and of fear of the Lord,
and his delight shall be the fear of the Lord.
Not by appearance shall he judge,
nor by hearsay shall he decide,
But he shall judge the poor with justice,
and decide fairly for the land's afflicted.
He shall strike the ruthless with the
rod of his mouth,
and with the breath of his lips he shall
slay the wicked.
Justice shall be the band around his waist,
and faithfulness a belt upon his hips.
Then the wolf shall be the guest of the lamb,
and the leopard shall lie down with the
young goat.
The calf and the young lion shall browse
together,

with a little child to guide them.
The cow and the bear shall graze,
together their young shall lie down;
the lion shall eat hay like the ox.
The baby shall play in the viper's den
and the child shall lay his hand on the adder's lair.
They shall not harm or destroy on all my holy
mountain;
for the earth shall be filled with knowledge
of the Lord,
as water covers the sea. (Isaiah 11:2-9)

**Maran atha**

# Epilogue

As you might expect, writing a book like this is not simple but it has been a delightful experience for me. As always, the teacher learns a lot more than the student. As I tried to look into the mind of Eleazar, I began to see the gospel stories from a completely different perspective. They are no longer stories that occurred long ago. They were happening now, in the present moment, my moment. For me, that makes a huge difference. It tells me that all the things Jesus said and did in the flesh, he is still doing. In other words, he really didn't leave when he ascended into heaven. Rather, he continues to be present through all believers. As someone once said, we become his hands, his feet and his voice. When we speak words of comfort or tend to someone's wounds, whether they are of the heart or mind or body, Jesus is doing them through us. When we truly love one another, sacrifice ourselves for another or suffer for the sake of another, Jesus is doing the loving, making the sacrifices and suffering again on the cross.

When Jesus sent the Holy Spirit on Pentecost, it was his spirit and one could say, in a way, it was his second coming. He could not return in the flesh else he be limited by time and space. Through the Holy Spirit he can be everywhere in every one. He is no longer an itinerant preacher and wonder worker in Galilee and Judea; he is millions, even billions of those. The stories relayed in the gospels are not meant to be left in a book for pious reading or limited to liturgy and prayer. They are meant to be relived.

St Paul understood this well. He called those in his community, *The Body of Christ*, because he knew that through baptism we are united to Christ; Christ dwells in us and his indwelling empowers us to proclaim the gospel through the good things we say and do.

Eleazar is not an abstract idea nor is he a semi-fictitious person. He is you and me as we struggle to understand who Jesus is and what he means to us in our lives. He is you and me trying to accept the challenges that Jesus presents to us every day.

In our world today accepting those challenges seem paramount for true peace and justice. I look around and see a nation more divided than ever. More people are caught up in a culture of lies. Few people seemed to really embrace gospel values and very few "love their enemies and pray for their persecutors". We need to be apostles, to spread Jesus' gospel of love and mercy more that ever.

Like Eleazar, we continually face the challenges of the gospel and, like him, we dwell on them, act on them or ignore them. Often, we don't want to hear them but again, like Eleazar, if we are true to ourselves and to the Lord, we will respond to the challenges of the gospel more often than not. And when we do, we become a lamp set on a lampstand, the light of Christ for all to see; we become to salt of the earth that flavors the world not only with gospel values but also with gospel deeds and we become the tree that bears good fruit.

We *can* change the world. We *can* make it a better place to live in because we can replace the lies with the truth, the cruelty with mercy and the hatred with love- the love of Christ, as we learn to love one another as he loves us.

With love and prayers,

Deacon Bob

# Bibliography and Recommended Reading

Antonacci, Mark. *The Resurrection of the Shroud*. New York: M. Evans and Company, Inc., 2000.

Barbet, Pierre, MD. *A Doctor at Calvary,* New York: P.J. Kennedy & Sons, 1953,

Brown, Raymond E. *The Birth of the Messiah*: *A Commentary on the Infancy Narratives in the Gospels of Matthew and Luke*. New York: Doubleday 1993.

- *The Gospel According to John* (i-xii). Anchor Bible. New York: Doubleday, 1966.
- *The Gospel According to John (xii-xxi)*. Anchor Bible. New York: Doubleday, 1970
- *The Anchor Bible Reference Library*: *An Introduction to the New Testament*. New York: Doubleday, 1996.
- *The New Jerome Biblical Commentary*. Englewood Cliff, NJ: Prentice Hall, 1990

Charpentier, Etienne. *How to Read the New Testament. New York*: Crossroad, 1983.

Crossan, John Dominic. *The Historical Jesus,* The Life of a Mediterranean Jewish Peasant. San Francisco: HarperCollins, 1992.

Fitzmeyer, Joseph A. *The Gospel According to Luke, I-IX*. Anchor Bible, Vol 28. New York: Doubleday, 1982.

- *The Gospel According to Luke*, X-XXIV. Anchor Bible, Vol. 28A. New York: Doubleday, 1985

Hahn, Scott, ed. *Catholic Bible Dictionary,* New York: Doubleday, 2008.

Harrington, Wilfred J., OP. *Jesus Our Brother: The Humanity of the Lord.* Mahwah, NJ: Paulist, 2010.

Johnson, Luke Timothy. *The Gospel of Luke.* Sacra Pagina Series. Collegeville, MN: Liturgical Press, 1991.

-    *The Real Jesus,* A Misguided Quest for the Historical Jesus and the Truth of the Traditional Gospels. San Francisco: HarperCollins, 1996.

Maier, Paul L. *Eusebius, The Church History.* Grand Rapids, MI: Kegel Publications, 1999.

Marshall, The Reverend Alfred. *The R.S.V. Interlinear Greek-English New Testament.* Grand Rapids, MI: Zondervan, 1970.

Mays, James L, ed. *Harper's Bible Dictionary.* New York: HarperCollins, 1988.

McBrien, Richard P, ed. *The Harper Collins Encyclopedia of Catholicism.* San Francisco: Harper Collins, 1995.

Meier, John P. The Anchor Bible Reference Library: A Marginal Jew. New York: Doubleday, 1991.

Metzger, Bruce M & Coogan, Michael D, ed. *The Oxford Companion to the Bible.* New York: Oxford University Press, 1993.

Milavec, Aaron. *The Didache.* New York: The Newman Press, 2003.

O'Grady, John F. *According to John,* The Witness of the Beloved Disciple. New York: Paulist Press, 1999.

Ratzinger, Joseph, Pope Benedict XVI. *Jesus of Nazareth,* From the Baptism in the Jordan to the Transfiguration. San Francisco: Ignatius Press, 2007.

Rogers, Cleon L. Jr. *The Topical Josephus,* Grand Rapids MI: Zondervan Publishing House, 1992.

Senior, Donald, Collins, John J, Getty, Mary Ann, ed. *The New Catholic Study Bible, Third Edition.* New York: Oxford University Press, 2013.

Throckmorton, Jr., Burton H. *Gospel Parallels,* Toronto: Thomas Nelson & Sons, 1967

Tremmel, Robert. *The Four Gospels.* Bloomington, IN: Xlibris Corp., 2010.

Wilson, Ian. *Jesus The Evidence.* San Francisco: Harper and Row, 1984.

-    *The Shroud,* Fresh Light on the 2000 Year Old Mystery. London: Bantam Press, 2011.

-    *The Blood of the Shroud.* New York: The Free Press, 1998.

# Map of Palestine during time of Christ

Used with permission from *The Anchor Bible Reference Library*